My Life and Experience in America

This book is an initiative of
The Odisha Society of the Americas –
New York, New Jersey, Pennsylvania
(OSA NYNJPA) chapter.

My Life and Experience in America
The Land of Milk and Honey

Memoirs of Forty Years
by Krushna Mohan Das
G.B.V.C. (Patna), P.G. (I.V.R.I.),
D.V.M. (N.Y.), M.S., Ph.D. (Cornell)

BLACK EAGLE BOOKS
Dublin, USA | Bhubaneswar, India

🦅 Black Eagle Books
USA address:
7464 Wisdom Lane
Dublin, OH 43016

India address:
E/312, Trident Galaxy, Kalinga Nagar,
Bhubaneswar-751003, Odisha, India

E-mail: info@blackeaglebooks.org
Website: www.blackeaglebooks.org

First International Edition Published by
Black Eagle Books, 2024

**MY LIFE AND EXPERIENCE IN AMERICA
THE LAND OF MILK AND HONEY**

**Memoirs of Forty Years
by Krushna Mohan Das**
70, Pinewood Road, Manhasset,
Long Island, Ney York - 11030

Copyright © **Basanta Kumari Das**

All rights reserved. No part of this publication may be reproduced, stored in a retrieval system, or transmitted, in any form or by any means, electronic, mechanical, photocopying, recording or otherwise without the prior permission of the publisher.

Cover & Interior Design: Ezy's Publication

ISBN- 978-1-64560-593-5 (Paperback)
Library of Congress Control Number: 2024948580

Printed in the United States of America

CONTENTS

1. Preface — 9
2. Acknowledgment — 11
3. My Life And Family — 13
4. Introduction — 17
5. Admission To Cornell University — 19
6. Loan Stipend Fund of Orissa Government — 23
7. Teaching Assistant At Cornell — 24
8. Organization Of Cornell University — 29
9. Emphasis On Research — 33
10. Student Life At Cornell — 34
11. Regular Hostels — 36
12. Programme For A Foreign Student — 37
13. Part Time Work — 42
14. Acceptance Of Foreign Students — 42
15. Libraries — 43
16. Living At Cornell — 45
17. Smelting On The Lake Of Cayuga — 50
18. Apple Picking At Cornell Orchads — 52
19. Dr. John H. Whitlock (DVM.MS) — 54
20. Dr. Charles G. Rickard (DVM. MS. Ph.D) — 54
21. Dr. Peter Olafson (DVM.MS) — 55
22. Dr. D.W. Baker (DVM. MS. Ph.D) — 56
23. Dr. D.W. Bruner, (DVM.MS. Ph.D) — 57
24. Dr. P.P. Levine, (DVM. MS. Ph.D) Professor Of Poultry Diseases — 58
25. Dr. Lennart Krook, (DVM, Ph.D) — 59

26.	William I. Genter	61
27.	Final Year At Cornell	62
28.	Driving Through The Countryside	64
29.	Picking Up Passengers On The Highway	68
30.	Racial Discrimination	69
31.	A University For Black People	71
32.	Return To New York City	84
33.	The Animal Medical Centre in New York City(AMC)	92
34.	Internship and Residency Programme At The AMC	95
35.	Yonkers Animal Hospital	97
36.	North Shore Animal League (NSAL)	100
37.	United States Government Service	101
38.	Living In New York Area	105
39.	Socio Cultural Activities Of Indians	110
40.	Blooming Burg Farm Picnic	113
41.	Oneonta Farm	114
42.	Canadian Trip Via Thousand Island Bridge	119
43.	Florida Trip	123
44.	Hunting	125
45.	Public Entertainment And Sight Seeing Opportunities In New York City	126
46.	Sea Food Market In New York City	128
47.	Long Island Beaches	129
48.	Maine Lobster	131
49.	Thanks Giving Day	133
50.	Barbecue Chicken And July Fourth	135
51.	Miscellaneous American Food Items	136
52.	Meat Production	137
53.	Meat Inspection	140
54.	Milk Production	142
55.	Immigration To America	144
56.	Immigration And Naturalisation Service (INS) Of US Govt.	153

57.	Educational Opportunities In America	157
58.	Business And Other Opportunities in America	163
59.	Opportunity for Medical Scientists In America	168
60.	Ways To Get Entry Into The U.S.A.	171
61.	Advantages Of An Indian In America	173
62.	Indian Consulates	174
63.	How Indians Succeed In America	174
64.	Why Some Indians Do Not Succeed In America	177
65.	Problems Faced By Indians When They Settle In America	180
66.	Problems Faced By Women And The Family	182
67.	Bribery, Crime And Punishment In America	187
68.	Income Support Programmes In America	192
69.	A Word About American Election System	194
70.	President J.F. Kennedy	196
71.	United States Of America, The Champion Of The Free World	197
72.	Basic Philosophy and Behaviour Of Americans	199
73.	Medical Internship And Residency	202
74.	Computer Science and Other Advanced Technologies	205
75.	Cloning	206
76.	AIDS (Acquired Immune Deficiency Syndrome)	207
77.	Soil Conservation Programme	208
78.	Preventing Loss in Storage of Agricultural Commodities	210
79.	Oriya Families In America	211
80.	Osany Scholarships	213
81.	Baisi Mouza College	213
82.	Americans Are Very Charitable People	215
83.	Go West, Youngman!	219
84.	Index	221

Preface

I found a gold mine. This is very far and located in a very inaccessible place. One has to cross the legendary 7 seas and 13 rivers to reach this place. It is deep inside thousands and thousands of acres of wilderness. It is guarded by a very powerful army of Super Men. There are many check points after the main entrance. At each of the check point the guards have the power of prohibiting further entry. If you have the ability and requisite qualification., you will be allowed entrance. If you succeed in your endeavour then you can avail of this gold mine of opportunity. You can avail of this wealth according to your ability and necessity. This is America, where I spent forty years. I have provided a limited road-map for people who are able and ambitious in the following pages. I hope you and people around you will benefit from this reading.

Krushna Mohan Das
Author

Acknowledgment

The following people were instrumental in the success of my career in America in some phases. I owe a sense of gratitude to them. Dr. J.H.Whitlock, Dr. J. M. King, Dr. Fred Tierney, Dr. Herb Rosenough, Dr. Charles G. Rickard, I'm specially grateful to Dr. Robert J. Tashjian for many years of collaboration and sympathetic understanding of my farnily situation etc. In the Oriya community in America I am specially grateful to Bimal K. Mohanty, Purna Ch. Mohapatra and Saradindu Mishra with their families for many social and other collaborating work. The visitors from India who were my guests along with my paying guests were great sources of social reassurance and help in many spheres of our family activities for which I am grateful. I am thankful to Mr. Madan Mohan Pattanaik, Ex-Professor of English of Utkal University for correcting this manuscript. I have a deep sense of gratitude to America and Americans for many acts of kindness and help throughout my life in the new world. I am grateful to those Americans who made my life pleasurable and successful. It is difficult to say that I did not have any unpleasant experiences in my entire life in America in my personal interactions but by and large the behaviour of most of my American colleagues and friends were of a highly sympathetic and helpful nature. In summary in this positive American experience I received more than I gave. I really miss America.

My Life and Family

I was born in 1925 to humble parents in the village of Chashikhand, now in the district of Jagatsinghpur, Orissa, India. My father was Bamadev Das, who was born after his father had expired. He had to look for means of livelihood at a very early age of 14 or 15 hardly after his primary education. He used to keep the records of revenue documents in the villages and also was an Amin doing land survey. I was the fifth child in his family. My elder brother, Khetra Mohan Das, is a retired Militaryman and my younger brother, Pyari Mohan Das, is an Additional Superintendent of Police at Bhubaneswar. My mother died of small pox when I was one and half years old. I was taken care of by my elder aunt, Sita Devi, who was a widow. I got local education upto middle English standard. I passed middle English School at Bagalpur with a scholarship, when I got admitted to P.M. Academy high school. Before appearing for the Matriculation examination I joined Gandhiji's Quit India Movement in August 1942. I was emprisoned on 9th August, the day following Gandhiji's arrest in Pune. I was confined in Cuttack and Berhampur jails for several months, after which I was released as an underage student. I appeared at the matriculation examination of Patna University and passed in the first division in 1942. I was selected by competitive examination and interview by S.

Solomon (ICS) for admission to Bihar Veterinary College, Patna. I qualified for a Bihar Government's scholarship in the first year of the Veterinary course. I completed Veterinary course with distinction and honours in Pathology and Bacteriology in 1946, when I joined the Orissa Veterinary Department as a Veterinary Assistant Surgeon. Sardar G.B. Singh MRCVS was my professor at the Bihar Veterinary College, and he joined Orissa as Director of Veterinary Services in 1947. He sent me for one year Post Graduate course in Laboratory Science to Indian Veterinary Research institute. In 1954 I was promoted to the rank of a Research Officer from the post of Veterinary Assistant Surgeon. I also held the additional posts of Pathologist, Bacteriologist, Parasitologist and Assistant Professor of Parasitology at the newly started Veterinary College at Cuttack. In 1958 I availed of a loan stipend to go for higher studies at Cornell University. I began my American life in September 1958. When I retired I was working as a supervisory veterinarian for the USA Government for the last six years. I retired because I suddenly developed a stroke causing semi-paralysis of my right side.

    I had taken my family consisting of my wife Basanta Kumari, daughter Prativa Kumari (Dolly), sons Akhaya Kumar and Annada Kumar to join me in New York in 1964. My wife's father, late Brajabandhu Mohanty of Nuagon Sashan, Dist. Cuttack, was a renowed land owner of the area and had provided much support to my family during my early days in America. Mr. Bibudha Nanda Mohanty, my youngest brother-in-law, who lives at Bhubaneswar, has been a great source of help and companionship to my family over the years. My Daughter is married to Ranjit K. Mohanty, IPS, IGP of Calcutta Police, the eldest son of late industrialist Mr. Naba Kishore Mohanty at

Jhanjhirmangala, Cuttack. My daughter has two children, a daughter Anasuya and a son Pradyumna. Both of my sons got medical education from Kasturba Medical College, Manipal, Karnataka and got their P.G. Qualifications in America. My elder son Akhaya is a specialist in internal medicine and pulomonary medicine and lives in Wapingers Falls, New York. He is married to Vaijanti, daughter of late R.K. Choudhury of Kheras, Jagatsingpur. She is a computer scientist and is locally employed. They have one son Krishna Kumar, one daughter Kristina Rupasri. My younger son Annada Kumar is a specialist in emergency medicine and surgery and lives in Manhasset Long Island, New York. He is married to Sanjukta, the Daughter of Dr. N.K. Pattanaik of Khuntakatta, Athagarh. She is a nurse. They have two children a daughter, Iris Yashodhara and son Amrit Kumar. They live in Manhasset, New York. Before l retired I had my main residence at this Manhasset house, where all the four grand children have been borne. By now we are all American citizens. Our decision to become American citizens were personal yet they help India in its burden of over population. We still love India and visit frequently. We have houses at Bhubaneswar and at our village.

Introduction

I became a Veterinarian, with a Diploma from Bihar Veterinary College, Patna in the Year 1946. I worked in the Orissa Veterinary Department for about 12 years before I availed of a loan stipend from the Government to go for higher study in the USA. I left Orissa in September 1958 and studied at Cornell University, New York, where I obtained Degrees of M.S. and Ph.D. While I was in the process of completing my Ph.D. Degree one of my classmates who was also in the process of completing his Ph.D. offered me a position of Associate Professor in Pathology at their college. The offer was for a period of 3 years at the Tuskegee Institute, Alabama at their Veterinary College. Although my plan at that time was to return to Orissa after my Ph.D. I was tempted by the offer of a rank of Associate Professor with a good starting salary. I wrote to the Government of Orissa to grant me three years leave without pay to enable me to take advantage of this offer as a practical training. This application was mercilessly refused by the Government, and I was asked to resign from the post. Subsequently after many more correspondences I resigned andcontinued my professional work as a Veterinarian and Pathologist in various capacities in the U.S.A. I held a variety of clinical, research, teaching and administrative positions in Veterinary Science in many Institutions in America. I worked for the Federal Govt. of U.S.A. for six years before I retired due to illness. I was quite successful in my many affiliations and I received high laurels in my professional activities. I was awarded the

Honours of PhiZeta, Sigma Xi and I was honoured as an Affiliate Fellow of the Royal Society of Medicine, England. Besides, I was a Member and Fellow in many honoured societies in America. I had a special sympathetic attitude towards my compatriots from Orissa and I tried to help them as much I could. I started a Society of Oriyas named as Orissa Society of New York which later on became an affiliate of Orissa Society of America and Canada. As time passed, my family roots went deeper and deeper in America which made my stay there permanent. My two sons who are medical doctors are also permanent residents in America, although my daughter is married in Orissa. My experience in America may be of some significance to young aspiring students who may seek their training and job opportunities abroad. The story of my life has been a very up-hill battle for developing a niche in higher echelons of study and professional activities abroad. In my life I have experienced severe handicaps on my path; - financial, ethnic and otherwise which are often insurmountable factors in Indian situations. I have experienced situations which would encourage young people to seek their fortune abroad because of a very unsympathetic attitude of the Indian environment. I have seen and experienced glaring examples of lack of understanding on the part of the authorities that may obstruct the ambitions of the young minds. In addition to lack of opportunities to prosper at home, there is added insult to the injury by a flagrant non-caring attitude of the policy makers towards the needs of the young people. My experiences in America have been very encouraging and conducive to growth and development of young minds. If this writing encourages a few closed Indian minds towards a more positive and constructive appraisal of America, I feel I have communicated my thoughts properly.

Admission to Cornell University

In the early and mid 50's there was an impetus for scientists from various Government departments for going abroad for higher studies as a part of the developmental programmes in agriculture, health and other public welfare areas. Particularly this programme encouraged young scientists in various departments of Government to go to England, Australia, Canada and the United States. There was a stream of scientific personnel going to the U.S.A. for higher studies under financial sponsorship of the United States. A few of my senior officers in the Government were selected to go abroad for higher studies. I was eagerly waiting for an opportunity for this purpose. I had an experimental research project of parasitic diseases of cattle namely Filariasis and Ascariasis in animals. While referring to some literature in parasitic diseases of animals I got a reference in a journal where some American made Filaricide had been used to treat round worms in people and animals under the name of Caricide. I tried to experiment that drug caricide as a treatment of ascarids in buffalo calves with some success. I reported this finding in a short publication in the British Veterinary Journal. The manufacturer of this drug (Lederle) praised my experimental results and asked me to continue the experiment further under their sponsorship for which they sent a large supply of this drug free. In this process. in my communication with one of the veterinarians in this company, I expressed my desire to go to the United States of America if an opportunity was available for further studies. After about one month of my communication with Dr. Johnson of Lederle I received a letter of admission for M.S. programme at Cornell University under authorization of Prof. Whitlock from the veterinary college. I was thrilled that

I got admission to one of the most prestigious universities in America without formal application. Cornell was most well-known to veterinarians in India because most of the text books we studied in India were authored by Professors of Cornell Veterinary College such as Dukes (Physiology), Hagans (Infectious diseases) and etc.

So, my intense desire for higher study appeared to meet with some success. I became determined to avail of the opportunity. Cornell University had not approved of any financial assistance for my study. So I tried to take a loan stipend from the Government. A programme of loan stipends was just announced by the Government of Orissa under the initiative of late Dr. H.B.Mohanty. I was one of the first few to avail of this opportunity. I got a grant of Rs.8,000/- of loan which initiated my journey to America. My personal financial resources being limited I embarked upon this journey against tremendous odds. This foreign journey dislocated my family situation. Since I was determined to go abroad, somehow I managed a few personal loans from my relatives and friends. My trip to America through Calcutta and Bombay was marked by expression of great enthusiasm by the Oriya friends and the employed labourers in Calcutta and the Oriya students of Bombay Veterinary college who were of tremendous help to me during my journey through Bombay. I flew by Air India to London and by T.W.A to New York. I arrived at New York airport, then known as Idle Wild Airport, booked a bus to New York City and another bus to Ithaca where Cornell University is located. An Indian student Vinod Kr. Bansal from Punjab also joined me in the bus to Ithaca to study engineering at Cornell. He also was tight on money like myself and we joined together in Ithaca to start our lives.

My initial days at Cornell was mixture of anxiety, enthusiasm and hard work. I joined the academic programme at Cornell University the following day after registering at the administrative building. To start with I encountered a tremendous bill as registration fees at the registration counter. Somehow I managed to convince the foreign students advisors' office, of the urgency of my need for funds and he kindly arranged my registration fees to be paid in small installments over the whole year. He also promised to write a letter directly to my Government to authorise me for some more loan stipend since the initial amount granted was not enough. After registering I met the professor who was my academic advisor. He was Dr. J.H. Whitlock professor at the Veterinary College. After I met him for five to ten minutes he wanted me to immediately start a research programme on Haemonchus, a fatal parasite in sheep and calves. He gave me the name of an author whose reference book was monographic. He asked me to go to the main library and get the book whose author was Barbarian but he had given the name as Bastian: and the name of the library was actually Mann Library and these buildings were located at least half mile from each other and I had to cover the distance on foot only. So, after making a few futile trips I found the correct name of the author as Barbarian not Bastian through the help of librarians in that huge library complex which had at least 30 librarians. I finally succeeded in getting the book I needed. I took the book and met the Professor after 2 to 3 hours. He was very happy to find the correct book and admitted and he said, "In my haste I gave you the wrong name and you got the right book. You are a smart man." He used the term smart "Cookie". This started my Cornell career with a mark of enthusiasm and appreciation.

The impression I created with my Professor carried me through my entire educational career at Cornell with great amount of success which made my stay there very pleasant. The first impression lasts long. A few incidents like these made my life at Cornell to sail smoothly. This Prof. Whitlock is one of those Americans who is vocal and proud. He represents a spectrum of American people who impressed me as carefree, of vocal, hard working and no nonsense type. I had a few more such episodes at Cornell which established that I was a very a sincere, hard working and bright veterinarian from India. Since Prof. Whitlock was of the vocal type he would often magnify my qualities amongst his professorial colleagues.""Once he had diagnosed a skin scraping from a dog as negative which I found was really positive for a particular type of skin disease. I pointed out that finding to Dr. Whitlock but not to the veterinarian who had sent the sample to him in the first place. With this positive diagnosis he would call up the veterinarian and the other Professors in the department to praise me as a good diagnostician. So after a few episodes like this my reputation as a diagnostic veterinarian was established in the entire campus of the veterinary college. It must be noted that the veterinary college was staffed by internationally reputed professors like Hagan, Bruner, Gillespie, Dukes, Fincher, Krook, Kirk etc. So I need not have to prove any more my ability as a student and researcher. It appears that within the first six months of my arrival I had established a very favourable reputation amongst the veterinary scientists at Cornell. This made my life easier and more comfortable. Dr. Whitlock recommended me for a fellowship from the University. Dr. Hagan, the Dean, endorsed the same application to the University with the recommendation that if there was one fellowship available it should be given to me and if there was none, one should be created for me. This was the strongest recommendation for a foreign student to get. So within about a month I was granted two fellowships by the University of which I accepted one which was more in amount. The fellowship granted me monthly stipend more than enough to cover the expenses besides complete waiver of tuition fees. This solved my financial worries and enabled me even to send money for my family maintenance in India. Within the next few months the veterinary college created a new instructorship in which I was appointed doing the same job I was doing before, i.e. instructor in Parasitology and Pathology.

Dr. Whitlock who was the chief guide for my graduate programme initially recommended that I need not take any course-work of study but advised me to concentrate on a good research project for my thesis. However knowing my own limitation in various subjects which I studied in India I proposed to my guide to allow me to take certain course of studies to broaden my knowledge. He appreciated it very much and helped me to select such course work as he thought would be beneficial to me. Some of the courses, we selected jointly were totally new to me because they were not at that time taught in India such as ecology, nuclear medicine etc.

Loan Stipend Fund of Orissa Government

This was a welcome institution created by late Dr. H.B. Mohanty of the Department of Planning and Co-ordination in the early 50's. Dr. Mohanty who was a Ph.D. from Cambridge saw the need of such a fund for the purpose of helping needy and desirous students to obtain loans from the Government for studying abroad in the subjects of choice by the Government The interest rate was very minimal and was levied on the granted amount after the completion of training period, usually five years. If the student so sponsored did not return to join the Government service they would be required to refund the money, otherwise the loan would be treated as a grant. Quite a few students who went abroad availed of this grant to make their lives successful and I was one of the few to avail of this. grant from the Planning Department through the recommendation of the Director of the Veterinary Services. I had been granted about Rs. 8,000.00 which was fully spent on my travel and one or two months stay in America. After that I did not need any more money because I started to have income in the U.S.A. enough to cover my expenses. I had some surplus money which I regularly remitted to India for my family expenses. Initially I was sending 22 dollars a month which was barely enough for their maintenance in my village. After about six months I began sending 120 dollars a month which was more than their bare expenses and would be equal to more than double my Indian salary.

Teaching Assistant At Cornell

On my appointment as a teaching assistant I started getting enhanced income from my instructorship. As part of my daily duty I would conduct a few post mortem examinations of animals, write detailed reports, conduct histo-pathological studies and present the findings to the second year and fourth year students in Veterinary college. I had a few classroom courses which would keep me occupied for about 3 to 4 half days and the rest of the time I devoted to my research project. I had to present a seminar on the consequent findings of my post-mortem examination to the undergraduate and post graduate students. It appeared to me that my routine work at Cornell was similar to the work I did in Orissa, under the guidance of Dr. G.B. Singh, the then Director of Veterinary services Dr. B.N. Rath, GBVC. PG. Veterinary Investigation officer, Orissa and also due to post graduate courses I took at the Indian Veterinary Research Institute. (I.V.R.I) The elite faculty of I.V.R.I. that trained me included H.D. Srivastava, D.Sc., B.C. Basu, D.Sc., H.N. Ray, Ph.D and Dr. P.R.K. Iyer. G.M.V.C.

At this stage I began to feel confident that the subjects I had learned in India were valuable in the international lingua. After the brand of approval at Cornell I did not have any more doubt in my mind as to the value of the learning I had acquired in India. It was particularly because I had practised those topics in my daily working in India. I would also confidently present my findings to the students of the second and third years of the Cornell University D.V.M. Programme. I would also confidently present my findings of the post-mortem examination of animals to the senior (4th year) students in the necropsy room. All these three presentations two in the classroom and one in the necropsy room were one-man-shows which I conducted efficiently. Very often my Professor would visit us in the classroom and stand behind me observing the class in progress initially unknown to me. The post mortem presentations were open to all faculty members where usually a few of them would be present and ask some guiding questions. Since all the presentations were in English, my being used to English as the official language in India was of tremendous help. Instead of my picking up the American accent they began to pick up and understand my Indian accent of English.

Each post mortem of the animal either a small lamb or a large horse included a complete examination of all the systems of the body with description of all the positive and negative findings. The report was dictated to the record for transcription by the office secretary. At the end of the report a summary of diagnosis was listed along with the list of tissues saved for microscopic examination. Such tissues were saved in formalin solution for histo-pathological examination. Usually there are three or four teaching assistants in the pathology department and the number of post mortem conducted by each veterinary instructor was two or three. This facilitated a detailed exhaustive examination of the body. Although there are no helpers for the teaching assistants one or more final year students would be available to help. The Head of Dept. Dr. Peter Olafson would invariably appear at the end of the day at the necropsy room presentation. He himself had been an instructor doing this for more than 12 years. Professors from many departments of the Veterinary College usually attended these necropsy room conferences. It was a great advantage for me to be appointed as a teaching assistant at Cornell University Veterinary College. Teaching Assistants continued for about three to five years during their course of studies doing M.S. or Ph.D.'s in their field of specialization. At Cornell, they do not insist on a programme of didactic course work for graduate degree like M.S. Ph.D's. If they think certain students do need some courses of study essential to strengthen their background preparation, the Graduate Advisory Committee consisting of 3 to 4 professors help the students to select the courses. Otherwise if the student was mature and had a strong foundation in his speciality they would not insist on any minimum course work unlike many American Universities. Such a mature student would be allowed to go into a research programme and do thesis for most of his time. This programme usually is finalized at the time of the qualifying examination. The qualifying examination is an essential part of a Ph.D Programme. At that time faculty advisors decide whether the graduate student will continue to take some academic course work before he enters into the research topic. They can fail him at this examination from the Ph.D Programme after complete analysis of his background or they can extend his studies and allow him six months or a year longer for another qualifying examination to enable him to fulfill the background requirement of a Ph. D student. Finally if they are convinced of the qualitative and quantitative preparation of the student then they will declare that he has passed the qualifying examination and allow him to concentrate on his research thesis. During this period of research the student will remain under his chief guide and continue doing some practical participation in the subject of his specialisation in addition to his research programme. Involvement of the graduate students is both qualitative and quantitative. The graduate students work at least as much as under graduate students. The day is very long generally from 8 O'clock in the morning to about 10 at night with a break of 1/2 or 1 hour for lunch and dinner. This routine is usually for six days, and on Sundays it is a half day after about 2 O'clock. The libraries are open 6 days up to 10 O'clock in the evening to facilitate research students. After the qualifying examination the graduate students in consultation with their chief advisor select the subject of their research which they conduct over a period of years. Unlike other universities they do not judge the success or otherwise of the graduate students on the basis of time spent for completion of their research. The graduate student is recognized and given extra appreciation if he has spent additional years on his research topics. He continues his research topic till he proves for himself and for the faculty, the ability in the area of his specialisation and until he has achieved some important results in his research. These graduate students are usually the Junior Faculty Members of the Department but carry on high quality research programmes. Their research programmes become the subject of books or monographs. These monographs are books reflecting the quality of research and teaching and academic standards of the Department. Often these publications are summations of the smaller publications in the scientific journals. The graduate students are not eager to write their thesis within a specified period of time and run away from the Department or College. Usually these topics of research become their life's goal and this is the speciality of these graduate students who become accepted scientists of the world. Many of these graduate students after completion of their Doctoral work continue in teaching appointments as assistant or associate professors in various colleges. These Ph.D's become the younger faculty members of the new department of colleges in the country. The Ph.D.'s of foreign countries who are already esteemed scientists in their own countries are given additional status for their achievement. Thousands of students from India and other developing countries usually flock to American Universities for such higher studies in variety of discipline. Such disciplines include highly confidential projects like atomic research with certain written restrictions on the participation of such foreign scientists. Such restrictions are minimal, but cannot be violated without penalty.

Organization Of Cornell University

This University is a combination of Private and Government Colleges located at several campuses. The main campus at Ithaca is in the central part of New York State, except the Medical campus which is situated in New York City. The main campus was founded in 1862 as a "Land Grant' College. These "Land Grant Colleges of the U.S.A. were the special features of most of the educational institutions of America. The Government by an act of congress shared their resources of land with the people to establish these educational institutions in various States. Since the founding of the United States huge tracts of land belonged to the Federal Government after possession of smaller tracts by private individuals. The areas which were not actually occupied by private individuals by virtue of a deed amounted to millions and millions of acres had belonged to the United States Government. These areas were called "Eminent or Public Domain" which meant supreme power of the United States Government. Such areas are usually more than half of the land acreage of the United States. These were forests, hills, rivers, mountains, prairies, etc. Only a small fraction of the entire land mass of the United States has been owned by the private individuals by any Government documents and the rest belong to the Federal Government. The Federal Government used these huge land masses to further encourage various developmental projects for the benefit of the common man. These land masses in various areas were given a title as "common wealth in the early and middle 19th century that is 1850's the United States donated huge tracts of land to form or found the nucleus of all of the State Universities in the country. One state University would possess several thousands of acres at its disposal. In addition, the State Government would provide a small working budget for implementation of various educational projects. In course of time other Philanthropists would donate funds for any special projects of their choice for any particular purpose. If the State Government or the Universities would want to sell away some tracts of land for cash to implement some of their educational projects they could do so. Usually one campus with a huge endowment of land was given to each State. Cornell was the land grant college of New York State. The name Cornell is derived from its founder Ezra Cornell who had decided to found an institution of higher learning where anybody could find an educational institution of his choice. The land grant supplemented the work of Ezra Cornell to found various divisions of Cornell University. At the time of writing Cornell has two major campuses:- one at Ithaca in Central New York state and one medical campus consisting of Medical College and Nursing College located in New York city. At the major campus at Ithaca the following colleges are located :-

1. Veterinary College,
2. College of Arts, and Science,
3. College of Agriculture,
4. College of Engineering (Electrical, Mechanical, Civil & etc.)
5. College of Hotel Management,
6. College of Business Administration, etc.

Each of these colleges administered the undergraduate programme. The graduate programmes of all colleges is administered by the Graduate School which has the final role of approval of any programme and as regards the course of study and their quality. The Graduate school is an administrative unit with a nuclear staff but has a roster of approved professors from the entire University. Only these approved professors can be accepted as guides for the graduate students. The Graduate Students have to select one or more of these approved professors as their guides. If the graduate students want to select some professors who are not listed as approved ones in the graduate school catalogue then such a professor has to be specially approved before the graduate students programme is approved. Graduate school only administers academic programmes. For all other practical purposes the professors in the various schools and divisions set the standards and quality of the research and teaching programmes of the graduate students. These professors who are listed as approved in the graduate school catalog are usually the final authority as regards in graduate students programme if they are the chief advisors. These are called major advisors of the committee of which there is one for each graduate student. These major advisors can decide whether a graduate student passes the final examination or fails. His decision is accepted by others who are minor advisors in the Committee. The final examination for any graduate degree is usually an oral one which lasts for one to three hours. In addition to major and minor advisors other faculty members interested or involved in the area of specialisation of the student are welcome to attend and question the student. The examination is a very informal one as is everything American. America is spectacularly informal in the implementation of any programme whether academic or otherwise. The examination is oral and not limited to any period of time or subject although usually it lasts for about 3 hours. During this period of about three hours it is a question answer type. The professors ask short questions and the students answer with longer answers. Other professors in the committee can question the a swers of the students. Other participants may also ask questions for clarifications With this kind of question answer session the examiners can assess the general ability of the students and specific subjects of his specialisation and topic of research. Some professors may point out the weak points in the experimental design of the thesis topic. They can also criticize the results obtained by the students as to their applicability as general truths. If the results of the research and experiment are not sound and applicable as general truths they may reject the thesis, thus failing the students. Whether a student will pass or fail is a judgement the advisory committee gives while considering all aspects of the students' ability, not only restricted to the result of the thesis. The announcement of the result of this oral and final examination is communicated by the Chairman of the Advisory Committee to the students then and there before the Committee disperses. Usually 90 per cent of the examinations end in passing students. Rare cases flunk. This is because the Chairman of the Committee usually decides on the thesis quality before the final examination. If in the minds of the committee members there is doubt about the ability of the student, they will delay the final examination rather than fail the student. Although the decision of the Special Advisory Committee is final a student who is dissatisfied with the decision can appeal to the Graduate School with his grievance. The Graduate School will in consultation with his chief of the Advisory Committee can schedule another examination. The result of the next Advisory Committee with appropriate invigilation from the Graduate School would be final. Often a graduate student appearing at Ph.D final examination is allowed to complete a masters degree but not allowed for completion of Ph.D. The intent of all these cross checking is not to allow an autocratic decision by one or a small number of faculty members in deciding the fate of a graduate student. Graduate students are treated as part of faculty.

Emphasis on Research

Cornell University specialises in high quality research. All divisions of the University are staffed by eminent scholars and scientists selected from all over the world although majority of them are American. One way of selecting international talent is recruiting from their graduate students. That means scholarly graduate students may be selected when they are doing their Ph.D. research. Usually, this is the norm for all universities but Cornell is more free to select their own faculty from amongst the graduate students. It is easier for Cornell to achieve these goals because each of the foreign students entering into Ph.D programmes at Cornell is advanced. The Cornell Graduate student is usually a mature person with many years of professorial background. This being a private university it has few limitations on who are employed on their staff and this enables Cornell to recruit its professorial staff from the international scene. When I was at Cornell many international scientists were employed at Cornell. As for example Hans Bethe (Nuclear Science), Ashdell (Physiology). Cole (Ecology). etc. I have seen many internationally famous veterinary scientists from all over the world at the Veterinary College campus. Participation of such international scientists give a higher tempo to the research programmes of the University. Very often such international scientists are only visiting professors for a particular specified period of time, six months or a year. They give lectures and demonstrations on their own choosing. They also conduct some University seminars which are announced all over the University. During my time these scientific exchange professorships included visitors from England, Germany, Sweden, Switzerland and Australia. Participation of scientists and teachers from Canada is considered routine and treated as a domestic affair. At the discretion of various professors research topics often included off campus affiliations with other institutions in the country or nearby countries and Islands. These programmes are conducted during the summer time to enable other full time students to participate. Contrary to the beliefs of some of us the productivity of such summer programmes are tremendous and end up in establishment of science institutes in various parts of the world. Cornell University also had a cooperative programme with the Orissa College of Veterinary Science and Animal Husbandry when a few students from Cornell came and spent sometime at Veterinary College at Bhubaneswar, under funding from the U.S. Government.

Student Life at Cornell

The University has about 12,000 students with 4,000 faculty and staff members in various divisions. The students are mostly in under graduate programmes with about 8,000 of them enrolled in various colleges, the rest 4000 are enrolled in the Graduate School for M.S. and Ph.D. Degrees. In addition a few thousand part-time students are doing courses in the summer time in various programmes. The students for under graduate programme are selected on the basis of high scholastic performance and staff recommendations. In America passing grades for a student in each subject is usually 60% with an average of 70% in the aggregate. However entrance into Cornell University would require a grade average of 85 plus per cent. More likely the students whose average marks is about 90 plus per cent is admitted to Cornell University. This is usually on a national competition basis. The University selects the top students in December (to be enrolled in September of the next year). However regular students are selected by April for the remaining seats which have not been filled up by highly scholastic students in December. It would appear that the total number of the new students admitted to Cornell every year is hardly 3000. Thus a large number of students who are eligible for college study are not admitted to Cornell, as a result of which thousands of students are left out of Cornell. This has resulted in the growth of a new University alongside Cornell University in Ithaca with the strength of about 12,000 to 15,000 students. This new University is known as Ithaca College which is located five miles from the Cornell campus. Cornell University is dominated by a number of Greek letter fraternities and sororities. These institutions are usually student hostels with certain strict rules and regulations and commemorate the historical origin of the student houses in Greece where all modern learning originated. The selection process to enter into these fraternities are very strict and rigorous and sometimes very punishing. The ragging ceremonies in modern Indian University campuses have origin in this Greek Institution. These hostels are usually small and they have some very strict rules and regulations for selecting members. They take a small number of students into their membership. These students are supposed to do a lot of Voluntary work to help each other and look after and help in the sanitation of the hostel. The expenses are smaller compared to the regular hostel accommodation of the University.

Regular Hostels

There are hostel accommodations for almost all the students of the University, say about 10,000 including the graduate students. Many graduate students are married and live with their families in the married students quarters. The student life is dominated by academic programme and athletic events. There is free bus communication in the entire campus which is at least two miles long and equally wide on the top of a hill. The hostel rooms are usually two and three seat accommodations. Each building accommodates a few hundred students in two storied buildings. In between residential rooms there are common bathrooms where a dozen students can go to the toilet, wash teeth and take baths. For a foreign student like an Indian using one of these common bathrooms is an eye opener because the students entering into the bathrooms are mostly naked. There are, of course, separate hostels for women and men students. Usually one or more of the senior students acts as a monitor in addition to a faculty member being in overall supervision. No cooking is allowed in hostels. The students eat their food in separate buildings called cafeterias. The main student union building provides a huge cafeteria which is open for students, faculty and guests. In addition to this there are several smaller cafeterias dispersed amongst these residence halls. Besides, there are small dining halls attached to each of these fraternities and sororities. Also there are cafeterias and small dining halls in most of the major buildings of various colleges since they are farther apart from each other. One of the major hotels in Ithaca area is located at Cornell that is known as Statler Hotel, which is also the centre of the School of Hotel Administration. It is one of the most famous hotel schools of America.

Cornell University is a highly academic University but they pay a great interest to athletics of necessity. There is a big outdoor athletic stadium for various sports events in addition to a large indoor stadium which can hold 10,000 participants. All kinds of sports activities are encouraged however, Cornell is well- recognised in American football and basketball. They participate in all other sports activities in American college world but they do not patronise sports at the expense of academics.

Programme for a Foreign Student

Cornell pays special respect and attention to its foreign student body. They select highly talented students from all over the world while admitting to the vacancies of only 3000 new admissions in a year. Usually they are about 10% of the total strength of Cornell from foreign countries. There are special programmes of orientation for these foreign students. Most of these students do not speak good English. Because of background of English language in India, the Indian students are far better than other foreign students in the language field. although they maintain an Indianised English accent for life. There is a Director of foreign students in the office of admission who helps in the orientation of these foreign students in their early days in campus. This foreign student office is manned by about half a dozen competent people with a senior administrator in charge. They are very helpful in solving day-to-day problems confronting foreign students such as language course, finance, suitable accommodation where these foreign students can cook their own food and do other activities. This foreign students office also prefers to have some foreign students or foreign born students and staff on their rolls. During the first two years of my stay I found the foreign students office of immense help in solving my personal and financial problems. This foreign students office helps the needy foreign students in selection of language courses, contacting the various faculty and students from the same country for social support and solution of any common problem the foreign students face in their early days at Cornell. They were helpful in finding room mates of the same ethnic and language background for the new entrants. This office conducts an orientation programme for foreign students during the early days of the semester. This orientation programme consists of guidance and presentation by the more senior students in the campus for the new comers. An important consideration for the new coming foreign students is financial. The older foreign students often guide the newer ones with practical advice to solve these problems, since life in Arnerica is about 30 times more expensive than most of the countries, This is a major area of concern for the new foreign students in addition to language. This orientation programme also emphasizes the student and faculty relationship where it is of a more informal type than in some of the older cultures. Yet a few features of American academic life stands out different and must be mentioned. Punctuality in the class room and various functions is remarkable. Truthfulness, honesty and frankness amongst the students are palpable. Students' evaluation of professors' performance is vocal. Faculty relationship with the students and their guidance and teaching are permeated by a deference towards the students. No spoon feeding is encouraged at Cornell. The first year experience at Cornell is a ruthless one where each one fends for himself. It is a concept of do or die. Since the students selected for admission at Cornell is of a high caliber this usually is not a problem for meritorious and hard working students. However, those who are basically poor performers decide to leave Cornell. So also majority of the mediocre ones. Only bright, hard working, talented and successful ones predominate at Cornell in various classes.

In summary Cornell's programme of encouraging talent among the student body provides intensive search for finding out and enrolling the talented students among the applicants. The principal guidelines for this is as follows: professors are highly talented and successful people in their field of study. They are also highly dedicated and some of them are internationally famous. The very nature and scholastic attitude of these professors are guides for the success of their class. They are highly disciplined. They try to instill a sense of perseverance and hard work in the minds of the students, yet do not put over-disciplinary concepts into their heads. They offer a large degree of freedom and informality to the students so that their innate ability can come to fruition. At most the fresh students of Cornell University are left to chart their courses of action. They are not immediately drilled to form a rigorous study pattern. But from the second year Cornell is not very sympathetic to the poor performers. They would rather see some of the poor performers drop out of the university rather than impede the programmes of the whole class. In the assignments for various small projects on which the Cornell students write term papers, they try to encourage students' initiatives in thinking with reference to the vast literature and make knew attempts to solve their current problems. Initiative in thinking and solving problems are encouraged by the faculty. In course presentations the professors only cover sample subjects of study in the particular subject instead of following the books page by page or even chapter by chapter. In classroom presentations these professors who are usually the authorities on the subject are helped by a few instructors who provide a class with written outlines of the course discussed in the lecture and also help students in answering and understanding some of the subjects discussed in the class. These instructors are junior faculty members who are bright and usually persons that have finished doctoral work or Ph.D. candidates or in the preparation for such degrees. These instructors are also equal in caliber and attitude as their professors. They would help but not spoon-feed the students. They would encourage group discussions on difficult subjects while the instructors themselves are presiding. Dress code at Cornell University is very informal in the classroom. Yet students are not very shabby in their choice of dress. Needless to say the class is coeducational and the male students are expected to be respectful to the presence of female students throughout. Cornell's professors have a special duty of being chaperons to the students in the entire campus. They can report misbehavior of any student anywhere in the campus. However this power of supervision of personal freedom of students is rarely used or called for. By and large the foreign students are more formal than their American counterparts. They are usually better dressed and more polite and less rambunctious in their behaviour. There may be a reason for this. Because most of the foreign students come here through a rigorous selection process by their Governments or Institutions and are more mature. Another reason may be due to their relative language deficiency.

Part Time Work

At Cornell there is immense oppertunity for part time work in the campus. The university encourages their students to do part time work and earn money for part of their expenses. This part time work allows the students to participate in various University activities and mix with the total student body. It helps them to grow at Cornell to be well adjusted adults. It also provides the students to expose to various divisions of the university and become more familiar. It helps the new students in gaining confidence in the campus. So they prefer to give any possible part time jobs to the students without discrimination to their national origin. They still remain within limits of the immigration rules for foreign students. These rules require that no more than twenty hours work can be given to a student during the school session. During summer time, however, students can be employed full time working forty hours or more during a week. In that period also the University professors employ their own students in any possible jobs. Cornell campus being spread over thousands of acres of land and having miles and miles of roads, consisting of hundreds of multi-storied buildings provide diverse opportunity for such students to gather experience in their own field of study or some other. The surrounding community of Cornell which is semi-rural is very receptive to the foreign students. Because they have been used to foreign faces for a long period of time.

Further, these surrounding communities are usually the homes and farms owned by Cornell faculty or ex-faculty members.

Acceptance of Foreign Students

Cornell is a very liberal university campus. The local community and the city of Ithaca are by virtue of their being located adjacent to the university, is more enlightened and liberal than some conservative campuses in America. There is no discrimination on the basis of race at Cornell and among the nearby communities. As a matter of fact thousands of students and their family members from various countries of the world add a cosmopolitan atmosphere to Cornell university. The very presence of such large number of foreigners is educational to the local population in becoming liberal. Growth of another big institution near the campus is known as Ithaca college. This college also provides opportunity for a large number of foreign students to get education in variety of subjects. This town of Ithaca situated at one of the lakes is principally a university town. The town provides business opportunity for a small community of about 20 thousand people as an outgrowth of this university town. Since both the universities i.e. Cornell and Ithaca college are private institutions admitting foreign students from various lands has made this area hospitable to foreign students. These foreign students are familiar faces at both campuses and the city of Ithaca. Various social activities of the communities would have participation of foreign students or faculty members.

During my time at Cornell I had the most enjoyable days in interacting with both the students and the faculty.

During the first year of my stay, I was little bit hectic but I began to calm down and became stable participant in Cornell's programmes in the subsequent years. I completed my Masters Degree in one year and Ph.D Degree in two subsequent years, thanks to the encouragement and sympathetic guidance of Cornell faculty. I was very happy and successful in pursuing studies and practical experiments. In general I got a reception at Cornell like a guest in various divisions of the veterinary college or any other school in the campus. The important consideration in the minds of various faculties or staff towards me was if I was a serious and scholarly student. Once that parameter was established, life was easier. I got full cooperation from everybody I contacted either in the veterinary college campus or in any other division. There are two huge libraries in the campus in addition to the expansive veterinary library It is a great opportunity and pleasure to visit and avail of the various facilities of these libraries. The veterinary library has more than a hundred journals regularly subscribed. Besides they keep almost all the text books in duplicate. They also keep large number of reference books in veterinary literature of the world. Cornell veterinary college and the library publish "Cornell veterinarian, regarding important findings and advances in veterinary research. This is a monthly journal and accepted all over the world as a high grade veterinary publication. This journal, publishes important findings of Post Graduate students' research topics. I was honoured to have published a few articles in this journal.

Libraries

There is a huge library called Mann Library in the college of agriculture at Cornell. This used to be the principal library of the campus until the founding of the Olin Library. This library employs about 30 people at any particular time on their library staff. The library is open for about 16 hours a day using two shifts of people. The newer library which was founded in the campus in about 1960's is the mammoth multi-storeyed building located in the centre of the campus. This is the Olin library. John. M. 0lin was a Cornell graduate in chemical engineering. He became very successful financially by chemical and pharmaceutical industries. 0lin donated huge sums of money to Cornell for the engineering campus and mammoth 0lin library. This library would employ more than hundred people at any one particular time and is open for about 16 hours a day.

These libraries provide variety of services and facilities for the students and faculties of the college. Thousands of books on varieties of subjects are indexed and filed. The students that have an identity card can have access to the library and their reading rooms. They can take out any book of their choice and read in library and leave those books there on the table. Those books will be refiled by the librarians properly. Each book and journal has an index card. These index cards are filed according to an alphabetical order based on the authors and subjects. The main 0lin library was a six storeyed structure and included millions of entries, books and journals. This library would provide a photo copying service, a typing service and review of literature services for a fee. In addition to a staff of qualified librarians, a number of students are offered part time jobs in all these libraries. Large number of foreign students are employed in these libraries on full time and part time basis. Many Indian students also help in responsible positions in these libraries. A concept of interlibrary loan of books and journals can be initiated through this library. In this process the library can obtain for a student and faculty any book or journal of reference from any recognised library in the world, primarily United States. Either the original publication or Xerox copy of the relevant publication can be made available with a nominal charge. There is also a programme by which review of literature in particular subject can be obtained from the Library of Congress, Washington D.C. and this programme is called Medlars. This particularly refers to the medical and veterinary research. With request from Cornell Library medlars search can provide an up-to-date abstract of literature on the subject to the requesting library. This programme is highly useful to any researcher in the area of medical and veterinary research. A few foreign students use these facilities for conducting their research. This method of inter library loans and medlars search are very useful tools to researchers at Cornell.

Living at Cornell

During the Ist year I lived in small rooming houses with common cooking facilities and common bathrooms. Most of the foreign students lived in this kind of accommodations at least during the part of the Ist year. Foreign students usually like to cook their own food in their own way. Indian students use lot of spices in their cooking. Other foreign students usually do not use much spices. Owners of these houses do not like this spicy smell of the kitchens, so Indian students have some difficulty in finding accommodations in these houses. However, some landladies who have over the years preferred to sample Indian cooking like to keep Indian students, One such lady was Ms. Emily, who had about 10 rooms in the whole house with three common kitchens one in each floor. She preferred to keep Indian students. During my time that house on college avenue became known as India House. Over the years she patronized Indians and Indian functions at the campus. By general American standards living of Indian students was not very hygienic. They used to live 3-4 per room and a few of them would join to form a common mess. They cook alternately and go shopping to the grocery stores jointly. They select food items as cheap as possible. One of them would be a manager for one month and try to economise on the food expenditure. We had a small mess in one of the buildings on College Avenue. This was 205 college avenue. Food items bought included all familiar Indian items and chicken. Chicken was the cheapest meat in the grocery shop. In those days in the late 50's and early 60's chicken would sell at 16 cents a pound, in the downtown super markets, the same would sale at 25 to 30 cents per pound at College Avenue stores. So in order to save money two of us would go to the downtown Ithaca on weekends to do a grocery shopping. At times we find good fish. Two of our mess members were students from Bihar and Uttar Pradesh and they would not eat fish. So we used to have fish only rarely. Fish would sell very cheap in these markets, as cheap as chicken. Carp (Rohu) was frequently available. Other fish will be common American fish: Trout, Salmon, Blue Fish, white fish, flounder, shrimp, crab and rarely hilsa (shad) and mullet. Hilsa fish was not much in demand because of its bones. A few Indians like Bengalis who loved hilsa fish at any price. In my early days at Ithaca we used to get Shrimp at very cheap price, a dollar for a pound (the Shrimp now has became very expensive and sells for 10 or

12 dollars per pound). This is perhaps because the world has developed taste for Shrimp over the years. Lamb (meat of young sheep aged one year or less) used to sell in the early days at 59 cents a pound. Goat meat was very rare. Most common meat was beef: next to it was pork. Pricewise beef was the most expensive and Pork was the least expensive of all the meats. Chicken and fish was similar in price, so we preferred chicken and fish selectively. Most Indians would eat chicken, some north Indians would not like fish. Bengalis and Oriyas love fish. We had taken one apartment (flat) with two bed rooms, a bath and a kitchen. We used to have five occupants in the flat, two per bed room, one in the living room. The bed in the living room was "temporary" according to the necessity of the occasion. Dr. Basudev Pattnaik and also Dr. S.B. Tripathy of the Orissa Veterinary college stayed with us in this temporary accommodation. This temporary accommodation would last for years. By American standards Indian living habits are not very hygienic and far from desirable. Yet, Indians enjoy their mess life in small groups like this. They are supposed to keep their beds and their rooms clean on a daily basis and there is a routine allotment of cleanliness of the kitchen and bathroom but this routine is usually not followed by some of the members of the mess. Only occasionally the cleanliness of the kitchen and bathrooms are done. Since our mess was our home we rarely make a big issue of the cleanliness of the place and leave it to the conscience of the members. Expenditure of the mess was very low. Everybody tries competitively to keep it low during his managership of the month, so much so that I remember in some months individual bill for the entire month would be 15 dollars ranging up to 20 dollars per head. This

includes breakfast, lunch and dinner. Rent for the flat was divided among the members would amount to about 20 dollars a month. So the total expenditure for food and living was about 40 dollars a month. Considering that each individual was getting about three hundred dollars a month, in form of fellowship or scholarship this was a comfortable living. We lived in these groups for about two years That is the 2nd and 3rd years, of my stay at Cornell. Dr. P.P. Jha an agricultural scientist from Bihar, Dr. Pathak, Agricultural Scientist from Uttar Pradesh, Dr. Basudev Pattanaik and Dr. S.B. Tripathy of the Orissa Veterinary Department were the other participants with me in this mess. We were of the same age group and were family men. We had desires to be economic and save money for our living. Hence we had much in common amongst us. Our incomes almost were similar. Initially we did not have any cars, but Dr. Jha decided to buy an old car and learn driving. He bought a car for hundred dollars and asked another Indian friend Dr. Ghosh to help him learn driving in this newly acquired car. After the first two or three lessons Dr. Jha became scared of causing an accident by his car so much so that he decided not to have a car at all and not to learn driving. So the car was for sale and he offered to me for fifty dollars if I would buy. I agreed to the proposal provided Dr. Ghosh would teach me driving in this car within a few months. To which Dr. Ghosh agreed. So I had the car for fifty dollars and Dr. Ghosh taught me driving every weekend. Dr Ghosh was supposed to leave for India in about three months time. So that was the time he was supposed to have trained me as a driver. But this did not succeed. I learnt a little bit of driving through Dr. Ghosh and then appeared at the Motor Vehicle Department. I failed in the driving test and then decided I must take driving lessons seriously, I asked an American friend who was a co-student of my class of veterinary medicine to help me. He agreed to give me the lessons for the same amount of money he was getting from our department, when he was working as a student help that is about two dollars an hour. That was Dr. John Perry Combs a third generation veterinarian in New York state. He gave me the training religiously and rigorously. He would scold me mercilessly, if I made mistakes. After about two months of training by Dr. Combs I appeared at the test for driving and passed successfully. Now I was a driver and proud owner of a car which I had acquired for fifty dollars. The veterinary college was about one and half miles from my place of residence. Thus, the car was very useful for me for commuting to and from the Veterinary college. It saved time and energy. By the time I had acquired this car, I had also been promoted to the position of instructor at the veterinary college. So financially it was OK to manage the car's expenses. I still maintained my daily routine of leaving for the college at about 7'0 clock morning and return to our apartment about 9'0 clock in the night. I carried some lunch with me and spent evening hours in the library before driving back at about 9'0 clock and have dinner at home. On Saturday it used to be a half day upto 1 O'clock at the college. Saturday afternoon was for relaxing. So also Sunday morning. On Sunday afternoons I would drive to the veterinary college campus and spend time in the library till 7 to 8 O'clock in the evening. Occasionally I would have social invitations from Indian friends and families and later on from American friends and families of the veterinary faculty. Sometimes, we would join picnics and other outings in the campus in the groups of Indian students or international groups.

Smelting on the Lake of Cayuga

This was a very pleasant and wonderful experience which I had in the company of professor Valentyne in the course of a class on ecology. The whole class consisted of about 40 students. Men and women were asked to gather at about 8 O'clock in the evening, on the shore of lake Cayuga where a small stream would fall into the lake. This was at the Toughanic Park a nice picnic spot during the day time. We had all been given instruction to come and assemble at this park in the evening with hip boots, and hand fishing-nets. There we were asked to wade in the water in the mouth of the stream and grope near our feet and look for any small fish. About 25 to 50 feet upstream where we had knee deep of water, we felt for any fish around our feet. Lo and behold, we would feel in our hands dozens of fish near our feet which were about six to nine inches long. We collected all those fish as much as we could within half hour and brought them out in the hand net. Then we were asked to spread them out on the grass and separate them into males and females. Then count the numbers of males and females in each collection and tabulate the results. The findings were that invariably the males would number no more than 10 per cent of the females. The time is usually early part of the evening to study the nature of these fish. One can thus decide where to fish for them for good harvesting. Needless to say that each of us had the few pounds of this smelt to carry home to cook and eat. Smelt are good eating. Particularly the females loaded with the roe. This was a part; of our lesson on practical ecology of fish. The studying of practical aspects of various ecological factors predicts good fishing areas and times in the lakes, rivers and open waters to guide professional fishermen.

This practical lesson on smelting provides an example of lessons of study in animal ecology. This simple experiment would provide various scientific data for further analysis and ecological summation. Taking the temperature, pH, and counting of microbiological flora in the water, where the fish are caught and analysed. These provided the guidelines for ecological environment of the fish. These ecological factors are compared to similar data obtained on another experiment on a different day. On this other experiment we had gone on a boat into the deeper waters of the lake Cayuga to make a study of the ecological life in the water at various depths. We would compare various findings of the environment and also presence of ecological members at various depths of water. Summary of findings have been of great significance and provided guidelines of various ecosystems at the various levels of water. Another experiment was conducted in the back woods of Ithaca and its surroundings spreading over the whole night. The class included about forty students, both undergraduate and graduate and about half of the class were females. A few of us were unused to these overnight camps in the woods and dreamt up romantic interludes. But there was nothing of the kind. The students were all busy doing experimental study on ecology of the inhabitants of the woods at night every fifteen minutes in groups of three. We would observe and count and identify the various animal species. We would also measure their lengths and widths at these times. These information are collected every fifteen minutes and tabulated. Finishing the study at early morning when the sun comes out, the data thus collected are tabulated and analysed later on by the students at their own time and presented to the whole class in the next meeting, which was usually the next week. Very important concepts are summarised from this fieldtrips and have great implications on ecological study of animals in various ecosystems. So Dr. Valentyne's class on ecology was no fun and games!

Apple Picking at Cornell Orchads

In course of my early adventures in earning money I along with an Indian friend went to pick apples. In the university orchards they would pay us one dollar and seventy five cents per bushel of apples picked. A bushel is usually a big basket of about forty pounds. In the first few days of experience I found it easy picking of the apples which had gathered on the ground around the trees but when the professor saw this he asked not to pick apples from the ground. They have to be picked directly from the trees and put in the bags or basket, which made my job more difficult. But that was the rule we had to pick apples from the trees and we must also pick ripe apples: those which were not very ripe should not be picked. You can judge the ripeness of the apples by the colour and also how easily it can be plucked. If an apple is not easily plucked, it perhaps is not ripe. In one bunch there may be only 3/4 ripe apples and others are mostly not ripe. We should avoid those. We go to the trees where we see that a lot of apples have fallen on the ground. Usually the weather is very cold when apple picking is done and the pickers use thin gloves to protect their hands against cold. But I did not have any such gloves, so I felt the pinch of cold on my fingers. Also I did not have proper head gear to cover the ears and head. So within a short period of time I would feel very much discouraged. This taught me to change my dress accordingly in the next session. Since I had classes in the morning at about 10 O'clock, I would go and pick apples between 8 to 9.30 and then go to the class at 10. Those days I had long hair like most Indians and when I went to the class room after apple picking I was not only tired physically but also had dishevelled hair which was noticeable by my classmates. Within a short period of time I became tired because of the hard work of apple picking, particularly in the cold weather, was difficult till I found some alternative work inside the buildings. A classmate of mine noticed that I was looking for part time work and suggested to me to work part time in the university horse stable. He thought in the morning it involved only an hour of work for me to change the bedding, feed and water of eight horses. There were many more students doing this and I had to take care of about eight of the horses. I found out that his estimation of one hour time was really two hours by me. However, in exchange for this hard work the stables provided free of charge a room with a bath and kitchen. This saved me the rentals of the house. So I opted for this, which continued for about six months. I was quite comfortable because I could cook my own food in the kitchen which also had a refrigerator to store food. This stable was nearer to the veterinary college. So I found it convenient. I got used to the hard work of taking care of eight horses, eight big riding horses every day. In my days at Bihar Veterinary college we had training and experience in management of horses and riding. Further when I went to the Indian Veterinary Research Institute for post graduate training for one year. I had practised riding during part of my free time. This experience helped me in getting used to the horses at Cornell. My experience with horses at Cornell stables brought me to the notice of several veterinary faculty members, who used the facility for riding and playing Polo. They appreciated my being a horse hand at this stable. In America everybody appreciates hard work. My experiences at Cornell included my special appreciation for the work and help I received from many faculty members. Some of these faculty members stand out in my memory not only because of their contribution to science, but also of their sympathetic dealings with me. A few such people were as follows.

Dr. John H. Whitlock (DVM.MS)

Professor of Parasitology at Cornell Veterinary college. He was a renowned professor and author of a book on parasitology. He was my chief advisor for my MS programme. He continued as one of my advisors for the Ph.D. programme. Dr. Whitlock was a capablé man, quite knowledgeable in his subject but he was reluctant to spend time in the classroom, while he can teach for hours helping individual student. He devoted much of his time in research on taxonomy of helminth parasites of animals. Dr. Whitlock was very kind to me and provided financial support to me through most of my time at Cornell through some of his research projects.

Dr. Charles G. Rickard (DVM. MS. Ph.D)

A Professor of Pathology, he was my chief advisor for my Ph.D. programme. An elegant and tall man with very pleasant and courteous manners. He retired as the Associated Dean of the veterinary college. Of all the faculty advisors I had at the veterinary college he was the most helpful and optimistic guide to me. He was a very broadly educated veterinary pathologist. He had undertaken special educational programmes at Veterinary Virus Research Institute at Tubingen, Germany. (Max Plank Institute). His scientific stature and elegance along with his pleasant personality made him very acceptable to the class and the visitors. He was teaching the main course of general pathology: both lecture and laboratory parts, which was the bulwark of veterinary pathology at the college. This was being taught at the second year of the DVM programme of the college. It was a great pleasure to attend his class. This was one of the reasons why I switched my major to pathology from parasitology after I attended the classes of Dr. Rickard.

Dr. Peter Olafson (DVM.MS)

Dr. Olafson was the Chairman of the Pathology Department when I joined Cornell. He was in his 60's. He was a learned man in practical aspects of pathology. He had spent about twelve years at the Necropsy room. He knew the signs and symptoms and lesions on all diseases of animals. He had an excellent memory. He was a tough administrator. I had Dr. Olafson as my chief advisor during about one year when Dr. Rickard was absent on study leave at Tubingen, Germany. Dr. Olafson was also instrumental in deciding to offer me a Teaching Assistant position in the department. When I had originally approached him for such a position, he had explained to me that he would prefer Americans, who had better facility in the language to man these posts of instructor. After six months of his judging me from a distance, he changed his mind and offered me one such position in the department. He is one such person who believes in the concept of "Show me".

Dr. D.W. Baker (DVM. MS. Ph.D)

He is a professor of parasitology at the Veterinary College. When I saw him he had been at the Veterinary College for more than twenty five years. He was in the 60's. He had immense knowledge of the practical aspects of many parasitic diseases of animals. He had personal knowledge of many disease problems in animals which many other Veterinary Parasitologists did not have. He would enjoy field trips and practical classes on the subject on informal setting. He was very undemanding as a professor. Many students would mistake, Dr. Baker's somewhat lenient behaviour towards the students in the classroom or the field as lack of knowledge or of experience, this was far from the truth. I was a student of Dr. Whitlock, but Dr. Baker who was a co-professor in the Department had let me occupy part of his office and laboratories for my use. He had even asked me to use some of the overalls and field jackets during his absence. He had plenty of these spare clothes and long boots in his closet. I was happy to use them for field work. As a part of my daily work as an instructor I had to conduct many examinations and handling of sheep, cattle and horses in the field during part of the day. These clothes and boots came in very handy for me. Dr. Baker was very happy that I was utilizing his equipment. Dr. Baker would remind some students as a typical absent minded professor which he was part of the time. He had quite a few thoughts in his mind while he was in the classroom. He would assign some subjects to the students and break away to attend to some practical projects on parasites into other Departments. During these periods of absence from the class I used to fill the void giving some practical advice and help to these third year Veterinary students, since I was a trained parasitologist in India, particularly at Indian Veterinary Research Institute. I found much common ground between what I knew and what was being taught there at Cornell. Indian Veterinary Research Institute is a high quality world class institution in these areas of Veterinary science. This is because of its origin and initial staffing by many famous British Veterinarians before India got freedom. I was a beneficiary of this experience. When Dr. Baker would see me helping the class he would very happily break away on some other projects. As a matter of fact my usefulness in the class was topic of discussion amongst students and led to Dr. Baker and Dr. Whitlock's recommendations to appoint me as an instructor. Since there was no approved position at the time it took some time before the university created one such position for me on their recommendation supported by the recommendation of Dean Hagan. Towards the end of Dr. Baker's career at Cornell he was drafted by the Federal Government for a special project of research and control of ectoparasites in sheep in New Mexico in the Southern border of the USA. His wife was a great hostess and very kind to me also. So also his Daughter Jeanie was very pleasant and helpful. I had many outings with Dr. Baker's family during my stay at Cornell. These pleasant outings with Dr. Baker and his family provided to me a sense of reassurance and belonging in this new environment at Cornell and I am very grateful to him.

Dr. D.W. Bruner, (DVM.MS. Ph.D)

Dr. Bruner is the same professor who authored the book on Veterinary Bacteriology and infectious diseases of animals with Dr. Hagan. Dr. Bruner was an elegant ex-military man and was an authority on microbiology.

particularly on SALMONELLA. He was very methodical and punctual in his classroom. He conducted both lectures and laboratory parts of the basic course of Veterinary microbiology to the DVM Students. He is usually in his class one minute before the hour, he closes the door of the classroom one minute after the hour. He does not determine late comers but there are very few late comers. He knew the details of his lectures by heart, because he has repeated the course for so many years. He is a kindly and fatherly man but he can be mistaken as an unsympathetic professor from his detached manner. I had him as my minor advisor in micro-biology during my Ph.D. programme and I had absolutely no problem with him or with his courses; he offered me all kinds of cooperation for my research work when I needed any. Dr. Bruner also was one of the editors of the Journal CORNELL VETERINARIAN, published every month. If a manuscript reached the hands of Dr. Bruner, he would make sure of the final action, approval or disapproval for publication within a very short period of time, about a month. His teaching methods were such that he selected his own instructor for the laboratory part of the class, according to his text. He usually selected 4th or the final year students for such jobs, although full time instructors would be available. Although he was approved guide in the entire area of micro-biology that includes viruses and protozoa. He only took graduate students in Bacteriology and left Graduate students in other areas to other specialists in the departments.

Dr. P.P. Levine, (DVM. MS. Ph.D)
Professor of Poultry Diseases

Dr. Levine was a minor advisor for my Ph.D.

Programme representing diseases of poultry. He was a brilliant professor of national and international reputation. He is a renowned author of many publications and monographs of poultry disease. Dr. Levine on poultry disease was so interesting and informative to me that I decided to take Dr. Levine as a minor member in my Advisory Committee. At Ph.D. level one is required to take only two advisors. I had already filled that by taking one in a parasitology, Dr. Whitlock and one in micro-biology, Dr. Bruner. I still requested my committee Chairman to allow me to have Dr. Levine representing poultry disease in my Advisory Committee. Dr. Levine was a highly learned man with acute sense of detecting signs and lesions of disease in animals. His methods of investigation of disease was very thorough and fool proof. He was non sparing in his critical analysis of thesis matters of Graduate Students. He was a pillar of strength and high quality in research programmes at Cornell Veterinary college. No wonder he was honoured to receive many science awards in poultry diseases. In spite of the fact of the eminence of professor Levine in poultry disease many students in his class would not give him due regard, primarily because these students were either planning a future in large animals or small animals, not in poultry.

Dr. Lennart Krook, (DVM, Ph.D)

Dr. Krook an immigrant from Sweden was a high quality professor of pathology. He was a tough taskmaster. He presented an excellent course for under graduate and Graduate students in nutrititional pathology of animals. He had many Graduate students working for him, since he had a large grant of funds from the federal government.

I was a beneficiary of one such fund with him. He was my thesis advisor in Ph.D. programme. I was lucky to have him as one. He drilled into me the quality of investigation and recording of data. He was a kindly man with a bright sense of humor. Once I had brought for a house warming party at his home a bottle of indian pickles, which was rather hot by Western standards. Dr. Krook called me aside and asked me "Does India use these pickles to kill the worms in the intestine ?" His course presentation on nutritional pathology particularly on pathology of bone was top notch and can stand any high quality appraisal.

A few words about Cornell faculty in general; they usually select many of their faculty members from the Graduate students at the University. They also have an eye for young brilliant professors from other Universities in America. A few of the elite young professors of foreign lands which come to the attention of senior faculty members through various channels are also selected. There is an interchange of professors between Cornell and other IVY league colleges in America. The salaries and benefits of the Cornell faculty were tremendously improved after the 60's. The location of Cornell is in a very snowy and hilly region of New York. This is somewhat discouraging for many faculty members. But those who are highly dedicated and scholarly, decide to stay at Cornell permanently and are provided with every opportunity and privilege for comfortable life tenures. Cornell faculty and students are alike an elite bunch. There is a saying that You can tell a Cornellian, but you can not tell him much. Cornell faculty walk through any academic forums with their heads high.

William I. Genter

He was a great friend of mine at Cornell. He and his family of four children and his mother and his unmarried sister were great hosts to me most of my time at Cornell, particularly after I had the use of a car. I was introduced to Mr. Genter and his family by Dr. Ghosh. Bill Genter was a farmer by profession. He was the manager of the Cornell University dairy farm, located about four miles from the Veterinary College. He had been divorced recently. He had a hobby flying light aircraft. He died while flying one such aircraft. He was a young man of late 40's and it was very shocking for me and all his friends and relatives to hear his sad demise. He had been so kind and helpful to me during my entire stay at Cornell, that I was feeling very close. like a close relation. I would spend many of my holidays and other spare time with him and his family. Once I had a breakdown of a car in the main thoroughfare of the University Campus. Out of desperation and not knowing many tow truck operators in the area I called him and he was there with a tow truck to pull my car to repair garage without any expense to me. Bill Genter was a religious man. He would attend Church every Sunday with his children. Although he was a man of modest means he was free on expenditures to host his friends. We had many occasions to enjoy picnic, lunch and dinner together. He was a typical, hard working carefree American who enjoyed every minute of his life. I really missed him very much. Whenever, I would go visiting Cornell I was confronted with this cruel reminder. I hope and wish his children are happily settled in the area of their choice.

Final Year at Cornell

This was the most hectic year of my time at Cornell. I was deeply into my research project, which involved taking care of a large number of growing puppies on a strict regimen of experimental diet. This project was to gather evidence of a vitamin, essential for Dogs-Pantothenic Acid. A group had been kept on diet with full pantothenic Acid dose with controls, which were on a diet deficient in this particular vitamin. These animals' progress of health and disease was observed over a period of months. Various parameters were studied to assess the disease processes in the puppies with the deficient diet. These studies included studies on the function of heart and other organs, blood and final post-mortem examination including detailed histo-pathological examinations of organs. I also had to work in the classroom and the necropsy room as part of my duty as instructor. I had already accepted a position of associate professor of pathology at Tuskegee Institute Veterinary college. So I had the pressure on me to complete the research project and also write up the thesis. Paramount was the consideration in my mind of completion of the Ph.D. Programme within a period of three years from my starting of the Graduate Programme. This, a self imposed deadline considered efficient in Indian system was in the long analysis not the right approach in the American situation. However, I had already developed into the Indian frame of mind, which would consider lengthening the period of study for completion of the Ph.D. programme as a disqualification. Under these circumstances I had very tough time during the final year at Cornell, meeting all the deadlines. The completion of the thesis itself, after the experiments usually takes about six months. This aspect had not been considered by me. However, I completed all the requirements for the Ph.D. programme by the end of September of 1961. It was satisfying that I completed my MS and Ph.D. degrees in three years time. which is usually unimportant in American standards. They pay more importance to what you did during your Graduate programme rather than how much time you devoted to do. In scientific and experimental projects they give preference and top priority to students who have devoted maximum period of time into this investigation. However, by my hectic self imposed schedule I completed my Ph.D. programme in October, 1961, but the degree was awarded in January 1962. I travelled from Cornell after the completion of my examinations and degree programme through many Veterinary colleges on the Eastern half of the United States to Tuskegee Veterinary College in Alabama, which is located near Auburn. Dr. A.G. Danks had provided me letters of introduction to the Deans of the veterinary colleges which I was planning to visit during my trip. Dr. Danks, a senior professor of the veterinary college was the associate Dean at that time and a letter of introduction from him was useful to me. This facilitated good reception and a guided tour arranged by the Deans of these colleges when I arrived. Dr. Danks volunteering to write letters of introduction to these Deans on my behalf was a very welcome help and pleasant send off from Cornell. A ceylonese (Sri Lankan) foreign student had accompanied me in the long trip from the city of Chicago to Auburn, Alabama, who shared the expenses of the trip and was also very pleasant. When I left Cornell I was very elated and proud of having passed the Ph.D. degree and also on my way to join the position of Associate professor of pathology at the other veterinary campus. The early days when I joined Cornell University had been filled with worry and anxiety and uncertainty; now I was a different person altogether. I was confident of my abilities and had gathered immense knowledge in my field and also was very confident of handling the position of associate professor in the new institution which I was going to join. The fact that the head of the Department of pathology of the Tuskegee Institute, school of veterinary medicine was also a classmate of mine in the Ph.D. programme made me more confident. The various visits to the veterinary school campuses in the Eastern United States where I received a very enthusiastic welcome also reinforced my feelings of achievement as a Cornell Ph.D., adding to my pride and satisfaction. The beauty of the countryside during my travel in the months of late September and early October was enchanting. It was different from India, which I had left only three years ago. The trees and the forests were a mixture of yellow and red because of the fall season. The fields were dark, green and miles and miles of corn fields ranged from brownish to green while driving from the North to the South. Roads were wide open and straight with multiple lanes of traffic on either way. Many big trucks would pass by us with a wave of their hands. First I did not realize whether that was good or bad, later on I was told that these truck drivers and car drivers greet each other with that sign because they think them to be their fellows and friends on the road.

Driving Through The Countryside

On the highway there are rest-stops on both sides to accommodate at one time more than a hundred vehicles and less number of trucks in parking lots. These parking lots were adjacent to restaurants which could accommodate hundreds of passengers in parts of the restaurants and at the rest rooms separately for men and women. These restaurants had both wash rooms and toilets in addition to separate rinals. All rest rooms were supplied with toilet paper and hand wiping towels always available. Surprisingly without any cleaning people in sight rest rooms appeared to be spotlessly clean most of the time. At the entrance of these rest rooms there was a fountain of refrigerated water for drinking. In the restaurant section there was accommodation for both cafeteria type service and sit-down dinner tables. In the Cafeteria section you serve yourself with your choice dishes on a tray and pay for the items at the end of the line to a cashier and then go to a table and eat. Near the tables there is an isle of supplies free of charge to go with food such as paper napkins, plastic spoons, knives and forks and liberal supplies of tomato ketchup (sauce) and several types of pickles commonly made of cucumbers. In many places you will find tomato sauce and other items in squeezable plastic packs. These are supplies which you can consume to any extent. At the end of dining you carry the tray with the dishes to a service area for disposal. Apart from the restaurant area there is the area where you get supplies of gasoline and other necessities for your car. There may be eight or more lanes for serving gasoline supplies for the cars. There is a separate area for servicing trucks. One can pay for the supplies both in the restaurants and car supplies by cash or credit cards. which most Americans carry. There is also a repair shop in the car service area where minor repairs can be done. For major repairs the cars have to go out of the service area on the connecting roads to regular service station. Apart from these multi purpose service-cum-rest areas there are frequent places on the road side which are called rest stops. These areas have no facility for gasoline or any other service for the cars. It has only rest rooms separately for men and women and picnic tables under some shade trees. There is, of course, a fountain of cold water for drinking. In most of these places there are vending machines that deliver cold cans of soda like Coca-Cola, Pepsi etc. and some snacks in small plastic packs. Within visible distance while driving you can see at various places some sign boards of hotels and motels even with their minimum prices. While driving from north to the south I could see the price range in the motels going down that is rates are a bit cheaper in the south than north. Also the rates are cheapest near rural townships than in bigger cities. The motels provide only sleeping accommodations with a few giving free simple breakfast. These breakfasts usually consist of donuts, danish and coffee. This is part of the room rent you pay. In those days when I travelled the room rent for the cheapest motel rooms was five to ten dollars per night. This is advertised in the big signs near the highway. These highways are typical roads that crisscross the countryside of America. These big highways were constructed in the times of depression in the early 30's to provide job opportunities to people affected by famine like condition. The roads referred to above are the national highways. These roads go from north to south and east to west, along the length and breadth of the entire country. They are numbered in even numbers going from east to west and the roads going from north to south are numbered in odd numbers. They are usually four-lane roads one going one way and other four lanes coming in the opposite direction. These have been constructed by the Federal Government and they are usually free ways. That means there is no toll to pay on these roads. They are maintained out of the tax collected as part of the price of gasoline. For each gallon of gas the dealers' sales taxes vary from five to ten cents which is about 1/3 the price of gasoline. All these taxes are finally payable to the Federal Government of the United States through big gas companies which are the suppliers of gas to these gas stations. These collections of gasoline tax are meant for building and maintenance of these national highways. More cars on the roads means more money in these roads tax funds, which is always in surplus. They amount to hundreds of billions of dollars. These expenditures provide for millions of jobs for people who work on the roads throughout the year. They make new roads, repair existing ones and clean the highways of dirt and snow. During the winter months cleaning the roads of the snow and ice involves big expenditure. These expenditures are huge which include not only the cleaning of the roads of snow but also spreading salt and sands throughout the roads network so that the cars do not skid while driving. America depends on cars so much that the money allocated for automobiles, their accessories and the roads are huge. The ancilliary industries servicing these cars and roads are also huge. The equipment for construction and repair of these roads and bridges are specifically manufactured for this purpose. They can remove huge trees from the road side, level expeditiously rocky soil and hills and level the ground for laying of road beds. These stretches of roads are levelled not by rolling a hand roadroller but by huge wide track rollers usually driven by diesel. On both sides of roads there are always drainage ditches for draining surplus water. Intermittently there are tunnels under the road to remove water from one side to the other wherever needed. Nearer the townships big highways provide exits to the local roads. Usually these exits are for parking lots and roads stops for trucks and cars also. The road signs are very elaborate and liberally posted. Exit signs from these big highways are marked liberally at certain distances at least about three times. Near the exit signs are always posted speed limits of these exit roads. Signs for the bridges, rivers, canals boats and ferries are also always notified prior to their appearance. So also the toll gates and their fees are marked on special signboards. If there is a toll gate for collection of fees they are manned by policemen to collect the appropriate fees for which they give a receipt. These receipts are printed receipts which are quickly provided to one without asking. If a car or vehicle passes the toll gates without paying the fees or without authorisation then the police may call on the extra personnel available nearby to chase the car and penalize them appropriately. These penalties are in addition to the due amounts of toll and can be hundreds of dollars with official reprimand to the driver. Usually after the toll gates there are a few marked parking spots for cars and trucks to make phone calls at the phone booths which are available. These phone calls can be on payment of cash (coins), credit cards or collect calls where the party called assumes the responsibility of the phone charges. It is, therefore, desirable that you have some coins or credit cards always in your wallet while driving. It is against the law in United States to have no money in your pocket or have less than five dollars. This law can vary from place to place and usually, are not enforced.

Picking Up Passengers On The Highway

This is usually discouraged and in some regions

legally prohibited. This prohibition is intended to prevent accidents and crime. Picking up someone on the big highways where the traffic is going at a very fast speed between sixty to seventy five miles an hour is obviously very risky. Also the person picked up on such highways could be a run away or a criminal who can do harm to the person giving ride. Therefore, it is advised by the police not to pick up riders on the highway. It is not encouraged at all for lone drivers. It is somewhat less risky if you have a companion or two in the car who could come to your rescue in case of attacks from these unknown pick-ups. In spite of all these restrictions and advice Americans do give almost free pick-ups to needy people on the roads. These people show their thumbs up if they need a ride and keep walking in the direction of the traffic. In some areas if police sees you giving such unauthorized lift they can give you a summon and penalty. Even on many highways there are signs prohibiting giving rides. It is not desirable to give rides at evenings. Always be on the defensive and careful when you are thinking of giving a ride to somebody. In spite of all these warnings I have often given rides to people who appeared to be in genuine need and I have never been deceived.

Racial Discrimination

In 1961-62 when I was driving to the south there was still evident racial discrimination in parts of the southern United States. These discriminations would consist of not accommodating black and coloured people in the hotels and restaurants that serve whites only. After a few years these racial barriers rapidly disappeared from the entire America under the rulings of the Supreme Court.

However, in the period which I am referring to the racial discrimination was still there. However, we felt we were Indians and Ceylonese (SriLanka) and we were not American negroes and deserved to be accommodated in the motels without discrimination. As we neared the borders of Alabama we were refused accommodation in one motel. However, after trying one or two more motels on the highway we were admitted to one. This was a bitter experience for us to face in America where we had not been treated as such before. Theoretically we had been aware of these discriminations but when it happens to you in person, you feel the pinch a bit personally. It is insulting to one's dignity to be so discriminated. But we reminded ourselves about how we discriminate untouchables in India and rationalize this unjust behaviour. We were stopped at a motel in Huntsville, Alabama which was deep inside the segregation zone. Alabama has a sizable population of black people (American blacks). One can join the black group and be accepted if his colour was dark but he would be discriminated in the white areas. After following directions to Tuskegee Institute Campus, I located my college of veterinary medicine and met some officials of the Veterinary college to help me to secure admission to a guest house of the University known as Dorothy hall. The guest house was sumptuous with provision for dining. The dinner menu was excellent and every where there were signs welcoming us as guests. I got the misunderstanding from these welcoming signs that all these accommodations and food arrangements for us were free of charge. But I found out later that I had to pay for all this service.

A University for Black People

The Tuskegee Institute in the city of Tuskegee, Alabama is a totally black university. It is about fifteen miles from the major state university of Alabama at Auburn which was totally white. Auburn university also had a veterinary college catering to the white folks. The Tuskegee Institute used to have about eight thousand students on the campus. It had all colleges except medical. Its banner schools were the school of veterinary medicine and a college of engineering. Almost all the faculty and students were black. Only a few faculty members were foreigners and white, so also the students. In adition to the general requirement of scholastic standards of college education Tuskegee Institute had a self imposed responsibility to educate the black community in general, particularly in the southern United States. Tuskegee Institute also was an active participant in the Civil Rights Movement of the American blacks under the leadership of Reverend Martin Luther King. This association of Dr. King with Tuskegee Institute had made the faculty and the student body very much aware and alive as civil rights fighters. There was a feeling of strained relationship between the white and the black community. Three fourth of the area of the city of Tuskegee was controlled by the whites and one fourth left for the blacks including the Tuskegee Institute. All important organizations and town hall were controlled by the white people. The white people would rarely come to the black area and black people would not venture into The white areas. White areas had many distinguishing buildings, roads, banks etc. There was a visible mark of discrimination in the motels and restaurants in the area, although public institutions, banks and businesses provided service to the black community with some amount of reticence. The residential arrangement for the blacks and the whites were totally segregated. So also the schools. However the white people employed blacks in large numbers particularly in the fields. They also had maids and gardeners from the black people. Black nurses would take care of the children of the white masters and accompany them to these schools for drop-off. These black employees of the white folks lived in their homes away from the homes of white masters. In the black area there were prosperous blacks, highly educated and usually employees of the Tuskegee Institute, living in newly developing communities with sizable homes and yards. Some of them also lived in the countryside with more expansive grounds. The countryside however was mostly an agricultural one. Life of the rural blacks even a few miles from the city of Tuskegee was a study in abject poverty. Most of these black people were agricultural labour and lived in humble wooden shacks. They perhaps had few acres of land around their homes and had large families. These were not the educated ones employed at Tuskegee Institute. These were the ordinary uneducated black people who depended for their livelihood on agricultural labour. About half the population of blacks in the rural areas were unemployed. A few of the women of these households were employed by white families as domestics. The white folks were more discriminatory to employment of male blacks in their homes, at best they were employed as gardeners. The women servants were more malleable and thus acceptable inside the households taking care of the children. They also do the cleaning of the clothes and ironing. Most of them are very efficient as household servants. They are almost indispensable to their employers. Except for the broad instruction from the mistress these black domestic servants almost control the entire household. They would entertain and provide dinners to the guests of the house and serve dishes on the tables always with respectable deferernce. At bigger gatherings which had more guests than the medium household, there were usually male cooks who are blacks supplementing the housemaid. These black male cooks could be husbands or relatives of the housemaid, rarely unrelated folks. For the white families to have picnics in the yard indoor or outdoor dinners in small groups, it is a sign of prestige to have black servants and cooks serving lunch or dinner. These domestic servants are often times dressed in starched whites and appear better dressed than their white masters. They would not eat at the same table with the whites. At best they will eat on a separate table inside the kitchen. They share the same food as cooked for their masters. Food is available in plenty all over United States. There is a noticeable drinking problem amongst the black households. Black families are larger and end up in legal or illegal divorces more frequently. There is evidence of promiscuity in some black communities. A more comfortable household may have more than one woman, one may be legally married the other may be a concubine. The black household usually have larger number of children born to the legally married wife or the other. The children are not properly cared for, they may appear ill dressed and unclean, but have to attend schools because of the state laws of compulsory attendance. Yet many children of school going age still play hookis. They have little landed property. At most they have a backyard, they are hand to mouth, there is no regulated life pattern for either the husband, wife or the children. Many adult unmarried children live in the same household. Many of them are unemployed. Most households in these rural poor areas have no cars or any dependable vehicles. If there is an old car that constantly breaks down. Alabama is a warmer region of America where winters are very mild almost like in India. So many households do not have regular plumbing or heating systems for the winter. They may have a hand pump in the backyard. Such homes may have plastic floor covers. Many homes have no running water. The floors are without carpets, some homes usually have outdoor toilets in the backyard in a corner with some enclosure. Most homes have a refrigerator and a gas or coal stove. Not of their own choice, such poor black homes are located away from the white areas. Although poverty is not restricted to the black community in the south, it is more noticeable, more naked amongst blacks in the south. During the period in which I spent about a year of my time in the south that is Tuskegee, Alabama, the rural countryside appeared to have a dividing line between the black communities and the white ones. Black community was marked by drab, uncared for dilapidated houses, roads, churches and schools. The white areas were brighter, well groomed, elegant and clean. The churches and the schools in the white areas were similarly different from those in the black areas. A few spots in these regions were marked by better homes and roads which were new developments occupied mostly by blacks that were better educated and better employed. In the early 60's prohibition of discrimination between whites and blacks had hardly begun in the south. The laws had just been passed by the Supreme Court against discrimination. But they had not been implemented yet in any remarkable degree. It would take many more years for that. So this is the picture of the countryside in the southern United States which one may not see at the end of the twentieth century. But the picture of discrimination and segregation painted here was real and almost all pervading in the southern states of the United States of America in those days. It was very uncomfortable and sometimes much more than that to lead a life in search of one's livelihood in the southern United States, if it was for either a black or minority person. People who have not experienced such overt discriminatory acts can not realise, the pain and torture, both mental and physical, one feels when subjected to these discriminatory acts. It could affect the lives of minority folks very seriously. It is not only a kick to the spirits of a human being but was an impediment in every action for livelihood of these affected people in their daily lives. A black person can not ride in the front rows of the bus, a black person can not go to the white restaurant for food, a black person can not go to the white school for education, a black person can not go to the white hotels to spend a night while travelling and for all practical purposes a black person was treated as a subhuman creature like an animal to keep its distance from the white masters. With all these actions which almost became the law of the land in these southern United States, these amounted to expropriation of privileges, liberty and freedom and almost equal to loss of one's earned property values in the affected states. If a black person who pays taxes for the roads and schools, hospitals and other institutions is deprived by various machinations under the segregated rules from using these public facilities, then this is nothing short of expropriation of one's property values under these circumstances. Even all these kinds of discrimination on the basis of caste, were present in India, racial discrimination stands out as different and more malignant, because it is based on color of the skin, which can be noticed easily by the person who wants to discriminate. In instances of caste discrimination in India one can not see the clear signs to discriminate a lower caste from upper caste, because appearance or color of the skin of both can be similar. In racial discrimination in America the color of the skin being black or brown stands out as an object of discrimination. The white man or woman how ever ugly or how old he or she may be thinks she or he has been born as a superior being. They have no tolerance for people of different color and different features. They believed in white supremacy. They believed God created these white folks after His image and considered all other races of human beings in the world as inferior to them. They believed in superior qualities and talents of these white races of the world to have been born with special command from the Almighty God to rule the earth including these other human beings who were nonwhite. In the moments of weakness of mind instances of kindness appeared to guide them to look after these sub-human races. This they considered a kind of duty and act of magnanimity. Through a large part of human history this philosophy has guided powerful races to dominate, subvert, torture and exploit the other races for selfish goals. Racial discrimination in America was not a solitary example of human discrimination. Human beings all over the world are utterly selfish and biased to their own kind. It is a sin God has tolerated long enough. There are efforts for removal of these sins from various parts of the world. I hope soon the human race begins to learn tolerance and sympathy for each other before they can even be sympathetic and tolerant to the non- humans as a way of such emotional tolerance is being preached throughout the world. Hope they succeed to be tolerant and sympathetic towards the lower creatures. They should be first tolerant to each other on this planet and respectful and sympathetic towards the cultures of other human races on this planet. Overt discrimination based on race and color which is still rampant all over the world should be rooted out, for making this planet a more human society. Martin Luther King was a desciple of M.K. Gandhi of India. He also believed in nonviolence like Gandhiji did. Martin Luther King talked in strong language decrying racism and discrimination in the humane society that afflicted America at his time. His appeal like Gandhi's appeal to the hurnan society was only acceptable by a few who believed in equality of human races in the creation of God. Martin Luther King was like Gandhiji of India, an apostle of non-violence:- one of the East and the other of the West and both were similarly gunned down by intolerant human beings who believed these apostles of non-violence were the usurpers of the privileges of human races which they represented. They took the law into their hands and killed these preachers of non-violence and made the world a more violent one. They did not realise that by removing these apostles of non-violence from the world they had also removed their own friends who would have stood in their defence had they lived. These violent men or women as in the case of assassination of Rajiv Gandhi are examples of extreme intolerance of human mind for other humans that express a different point of view. Martin Luther King was M.K. Gandhi of America. He stood for remedy of the unjust acts of human beings against other human beings. He stood for removal of the dark glasses from the eyes of the bigots and intolerants. He wanted to give a chance to these landless, homeless, jobless, uneducated, unemployed, hungry minority of human beings achance for survival and a modest prosperity to be able to participate in the entire human society on equal basis. He wanted to prove to the world, that the American negro who was in the present sad state of economy and intellectual abyss was not due to his own inborn faults but as a matter of conspiracy and discrimination on a huge scale all over the world and more specifically in the USA. He wanted to call to attention of human society in America and abroad the injustice and atrocities inflicted upon the American negroes by the white dominated society, in spite of the fact a large number of folk in the white society did not mean to do this kind of harm and damage to the minority black community in America.

It was highly gratifying for me to be coming to an institution of faculty position which had these high human rights goal not only for America but for the whole world. I had been a follower of Gandhiji since my childhood. I embraced a prison term in Cuttack in 1942 during the Quit India Movement, the day after Gandhiji was taken as a prisoner along with all members of the Congress Working Committee. I felt very proud to have participated in this freedom struggle of India in 1942 as I felt proud to join this black institution in the south of United States, which had the history of Civil Rights Movement in its background. I thought I had joined the right institution to serve the right cause. Tuskegee Institute stood for the education and upliftment of the underprivileged students of the southern black. I thought I would contribute my two pennies to this noble cause on a world wide scale. The people who built up this institution on the earlier days were people of immense compassion for the entire human race and they were determined to struggle for equality of human beings across race and national barriers. These people had made immense personal sacrifices for the cause by their actions. They had aroused a sense of pride and equality amongst minority folks who had been underprivileged, downtrodden and exploited beyond imagination over centuries. These leaders who initiated these Civil Rights Movements before Martin Luther King, were doing this, at the expense of their own prosperity and safety of their kith and kin. They brought to the limelight the various acts of discrimination by the majority community against the minorities. They graphically showed instances of abject torture and inhuman exploitation of the black people by the white over a period of centuries starting from the Africa's slave trade. They also provided opportunity for the new generation of blacks, evidence of these tortures on the soils of America, particularly in the south. Some of these memories are still vivid in the mürals and monuments of slave quarters in some of the southern states. Some historical documents of physical torture of the black people in the hands of their white masters were very pathetic and unbelievable in their history of human civilization. The black person was considered in the earlier days as a legal possession of the white masters and any physical abuse and tortures were considered legal until the act of civil rights by the Supreme Court in 1956. A few southern museums still preserve today the various evidences of slave trade and torture for historical purposes. The educational institutions like Tuskegee Institute were in the forefront of arousing consciousness of civil rights amongst the black. Particularly the educated black felt like opening their eyes when they used to read the history of the black man's progress over the previous two centuries. They followed these paths of slave trade from the wooded countrysides of Africa, the ships carrying human cargo of negroes, some in shackles of iron in the holds of ships. Landings on the shores of America and holding monthly or weekly auctions of these black people like animals are evidenced from the present records of history. The buyers of these black people had complete rights over the body and soul of these black people. They did whatever they wanted to these negroes. These black possessions of the white folks were not allowed to be educated. They were not given the minimum of human privileges. The healthy and muscular ones were the pampered possessions and were more fit for physical labour in the fields or in the households. The less fit and unhealthy ones died by natural selection beginning from the catchment areas in Africa, in the ships in the unhealthy dungeons and in the United States and in the hands of the new buyers. Some sickened and died with minimal of medical care. Only the strong and healthy survived and would be encouraged by the masters to be the bosses of their groups as long as they obeyed the orders of the masters. These super healthy negroes would be allowed to procreate their own kind and may have multiple wives although not legally. Legality was left to the judgement of the white who also took privileges on the female possession of these able bodied negroes whenever it suited their fancy. Thus you see dilution of colour in present generation of negroes which can range from black to almost white in the colour of the progeny. Some of these progeny of the white and black can be seen conspicuously in the south. The colour of the skin is almost white but the hair on the head is curly and kinky with other negroid features on the face, lips and teeth. Although these almost white people are different in looks from the generally black population yet they are also considered black by the majority white community. Thus discrimination on the basis of colour and other features of black people is easier. That means such people can be identified as originating from black people, although they are not black in colour. There is a sizable segment of this type of people of mixed-colour in the south particularly when you go to the southern borders of United States.

So in the atmosphere of these black educational institutions the reminder of their being the minorities and discriminated having a past history of having been subject to racial exploitations are constant reminders to these young minds. Thus it is very difficult for young black people to forget the knowledge of the history of their ill treatment in the hands of the white people. They are rebellious to accept the status/quo. They rebel first to accept; then they rebel to remove instances of such overt discrimination. In this process of taking remedial actions they cause more discriminative actions to the white majority to assert their own equality with them. They call these Civil Rights. We call them Civil rights too. But it is a very pinching slap on the face of the people who have been perpetuating it over decades and perhaps centuries in different garbs and different situations. It may be pinching and insulting to remind these cases of injustices and unfair acts but these are facts which the human society of twentieth century cannot stand. The present generations of human beings all over the world are willing to remedy these wrongs wherever they may be committed. The present day America is an ideal exercise in that direction. They have come a long way to remedy these unjust inhuman discriminatory acts towards humanity. But a note of warning must be sounded that even at the end of this twentieth century on a worldwide basis discrimination amongst human races is not over, and it still exists to a smaller extent all over the world.

Tuskegee Institute while adding its voice against human discrimination and segregation has pushed these measures far behind, but have not succeeded to wipe out the mistrust and lack of love and respect amongst various races. But it has helped the cause to a great extent. It has helped in two ways. It has vocalized the opposition to discrimination as a humans right violation, but at the same time it has also educated and polished the masses of black people by causing advancement in their general education. It has tried to maintain standards of higher education conforming to the needs of the universities and learned professions. At the same time it has also tried to bring up generations of less educated young people from amongst blacks to the levels of acceptance by the higher university standards of American education. It has achieved these by remedial programmes for the emerging classes of black youths. They have five year programmes for such students who need extra time and education to complete the usual four year degrees. Teachers are encouraged to provide remedial classes for needy students. Although the tuition and fees at the Tuskegee Institute are comparatively less than normal the University also has work through programmes. This work through programme enables needy students to work part of their time to earn money for their maintenance. Every University in America has programme for students to do part time work, so that they can earn part of their expenses. Tuskegee Institute does a little bit more in this direction. It tries to employ as many students as possisble in their work before employing outsiders. There are also provisions for a large number of scholarships and fellowships to be granted to deserving students under various state and federai programmes. The loan programmes established by the United States government enables college going students to take loans from the banks and the government directly which can be paid back after they complete their college education and after they get some employment. These programmes are also available at Tuskegee. There are special scholarships and loan programmes available for minority students which are available here. In addition to this many black philanthropists have established scholarships and other charitable funds to provide funding for deserving students. The women students are special beneficiaries of certain scholarships and loans by Government and various philanthropic organisations. If a student is admitted to Tuskegee and is in genuine need of financial support, he usually can qualify for this under one of these many programmes mentioned above.

There is also a programme for helping out students whose grades are poorer than the college accepts. Such students can be enrolled in some remedial classes and improve their grades to the acceptable levels of the University. Then they are accepted as regular students. Vocational schools at the campus are the schools of engineering, nursing and veterinary medicine. At my time there was no medical school in the campus. But there was a huge veterans hospital in a nearby campus. This is a federal medical centre where the past members of the armed forces and their families are provided treatment free of cost by the United States Government. Since the black people joined the armed forces in large numbers, this huge medical facility became virtually a black medical centre. Although there was no medical school in the campus of Tuskegee Institute there were a few black universities with medical colleges. One was Howard University Medical School and the other Meharry Medical College, which were not too far off. Therefore, the Tuskegee Students if they are desirous and eligible to enter into medical schools, these two institutions provide primary opportunity for them. I left Tuskegee much before the expiry of my contract. I left at the end of one year when I had a contact for three years. I decided to take this action because of two factors, which I confronted after I started at Tuskegee. One was a palpable racial tension between the white and the black and I could not be identified solidly with one group or the other and I was in the middle. The second instance was accidental. This accident was caused by my apartment being burnt down while I was travelling in Florida which was not too far. The second incident that is the fire in my apartment discouraged me very much and reminded me of my acute loneliness on my return. Thus, I decided to cut short my contract of appointment in consultation with the Dean of the veterinary college to which he agreed under the circumstances. I had been too spoilt in the liberal atmosphere of the North. I could not put up with the discriminatory acts in the south. Through my contacts with the professors at Cornell I got an offer of appointment at the Animal Medical Centre in New York City with a higher salary. And I happily accepted.

Return To New York City

This time it was a prolonged and extensive experience in New York city where the Animal Medical Centre was located and I got the appointment as a Pathologist. The appointment was for a period of three years with possibility of a longer period as mentioned over the phone. Very often appointments and offers are made over telephone in America. Things are very informally done in most of the instances except when the appointments are with the federal or State Governments or other big employers. In such instances appointment contracts with terms and conditions in detail are made. With my experience in India that everything has to be given in writing. I requested the Animal Medical Centre, New York to give me the offer of employment in writing which they complied happily. The Director was Dr. John Beck, who consulted Dr. Marshack of Pennsylvania. University Veterinary College and also the Dean of the Cornell Veterinary College before making the offer. At this time the Dean of the Cornell Veterinary College was Dr. George Poppensiek, who had replaced Dean William Hagan who had been appointed as the Director of the newly established National Animal Diesases Laboratory in Iowa. Dr. Poppensiek had known me for about a year at Cornell when I completed my Ph.D. programme and happily had recommended me for the position of Pathologist of the Animal Medical Centre I was to replace a famous Veterinary Pathologist Dr. D.L. Coffin who had gone on to a new appointment. The Animal Medical Centre also had plans for holding an International Conference on comparative pathology in the months of September of the same year. They wanted an important name to fill the vacancy caused by Dr. Coffin's departure. Dr. Coffin is the same man who had written a book on clinical veterinary pathology which was a sort of a standard text of clinical pathology all over the world at that time. In New York city I appreared to be a small fry in a big pond. Dr. Beck had made some arrangements with a west side hotel for me to stay. After visiting the hotel I found a YMCA hostel near by, almost infront of this hotel with rooming facilities for very small sums of money which were a fraction of the cost of the hotel. It was two dollars a day at the YMCA. So I opted for the YMCA hostel. This YMCA hostel had facilities for accommodating several hundred people in invidual and double rooms with many common baths. There was a huge cafeteria on the ground floor. There were also facilities for indoor games and gymnasium activities of the inmates. In adition to this there were other services available like in a residential hotel like laundry facilities, drug store, general store etc. A typing service was available for a fee. The YMCA the Young Men's Christian Association possibly originated as a religious endeavor, but now is a social and cultural organization for providing very inexpensive accommodation for transient visitors both young and old men and women without any colour discrimination. Providing a single room with all the other ancillary facilities for two dollars a night is the chief feature of this hostel. Food was moderately cheap but clean and hygienic. I believe I stayed in the YMCA for several months before I got a suitable apartment within my financial limits in the upper east side. This apartment was located on the east side of Manhattan, which was a few blocks from the Gracie Mansion, the official residence of the Mayor of New York city. The Mayor of New York city is usually a very powerful person. He must be not only a capable politician and administrator but also a person who has mass- appeal for the people of New York who vote for him every four years. New York city voters are very conscious of their rights and privileges. They are very demanding for the services due to them. They are very vocal critics of the municipal Government which the Mayor represents. The newspapers are published in the New York city provide good forum for these opinions. The New York, city resident is usually very enlightened citizen, conscious of his rights and privileges. They are also tolerant towards other racial groups, whom they see in the streets on a regular basis., New York city is a microcosm of the entire human society of the world. All types of humans are present in New York city in small or large numbers. While people of New York city are tolerant of each other to a point, they are also vocal critics of each other whenever the situation arises. Roughly speaking the city has 1/3 of the population as whites, another 1/3 as blacks and the rest 1/3 a mixture of all the other minorities. On an ethnic basis, Jews and Italians will perhaps be equal in number as city residents. There were areas of the city which were predominantly populated by one group or the other but not strictly so. These areas of ethnic dominant groups are by natural selection not by any means of segregation. However, on economic basis many areas remain segregated visually. A few areas where blacks are the dominant population are the Harlem, south Jamaica in Queens and some parts of Bronx.

New York city comprises five boroughs (districts). They are named Manhattan, Queens, Bronx, Brooklyn and Staten Island. These five boroughs together have more people than the rest of New York state or at least equal. New York city has a Mayor supported by a city council. The five boroughs have each also an elected chief called borough president supported by a borough council. Each borough is highly populous and can be a major city by itself. Each borough has about two million or more people residing in it. The borough of Brooklyn is the most populous of the five boroughs. The borough of Queens is more expansive. The borough of Manhattan is the smallest in size and area, but is the most important of all the five boroughs. This is the nerve centre of the city of New York and the state of

New York. This is also the commercial capital of the United States and the world. If there is any business in the United States or the world important enough for worldwide consideration, they have to keep their offices in New York city. The United Nations is located in Manhattan which was made possible by donation of a large tract of land on the eastern side of Manhattan by the Rockefeller family. The famous Wall Street which controls the business of the world is located in the down-town Manhattan. The statue of Liberty, a big monolithic statue of a lady, named Liberty was presented to America by the French and is located on the southern tip of Manhattan Island. The Statue of Liberty which stands for personal liberty and freedom of mankind is the Bible of America. Many Great Educational and Research Centres in Science, humanities and Medicine are in the Manhattan Island, such as Columbia University, Rockefeller University, and many Medical colleges etc. The foremost research centre and clinical hospital for cancer is located in Manhattan Island that is the Sloan-Kettering Institute of Cancer Research. The world famous theatre districts of the English speaking world is located in Manhattan. So also many centres of performing arts are in Manhattan Island. It will be an understatement of facts if one does not mention New York city as one of the capitals of vices of human race. Homosexuality, prostitution, drug addiction, high incidences of AIDS are common findings in Manhattan and some other areas of New York City. There is some relationship between AIDS and people in the performing arts area. Since Manhattan has a large number of talented Artists in the performing arts, AIDs and homosexuality are found more commonly amongst them. Many prosperous addicts among performers have liberally donated to the cause of research on AIDS and drug addiction. Many such foundations are located in Manhattan which emphasise research on AIDS. Large number of famous families of American society inhabit all round Manhattan Island. Some of them live in expansive villages in Long Island or up-state New York. They are the important people of America historically and socially. There is a society named Society of New York. This society has memberships belonging to these rich and famous American families. It produces its membership lists & sketches of the family history in form of books, which may be several volumes. These books are called New York Social Register. If there is a VIP in New York area, he or she is usually listed in these books. The people who are listed in this book take great care that their names stay included in this Register. It is a sign of great prestige in New York. I believe similar registers are found in many big old cities of America. People whose names are found in this society's directory are usually millionaires & multi-millionaires and well-known across America or even the world. They are known for the various charitable foundations they support. These charitable foundations have created huge institutions in America in various phases of social service. These foundations are listed in several volumes of books which are called "Foundation Directories' which list thousands of them. These are important in American society, because they have enabled educational, research, medical & other social service institutions, big & small to exist. Sloan Ketering Institute for Cancer Research is an example of such a charitable institution. In summary all good things and all bad things of the world are concentrated in the Island of Manhattan. You have to choose what you want. If you want good things they are available, if you want bad things they are also available.

Communication centre of the world is located also in New York City. The New York Airport which is known as Kennedy International Airport, was known as Idle Wild Airport when I arrived in 1958 and is a part of New York city. All the train communication to the rest of America and all the buses connecting the rest of America are located in the Manhattan Island. So also the international ocean liners located in the Manhattan Island. So if the Manhattanites thought that God created the Manhattan Island in His image, he was not too far wrong. The boroughs of New York city are outgrowths of the activities in Manhattan. There has been some dispersion of activities from Manhattan to other boroughs and some concentration of activities of other boroughs in Manhattan. For example the administrative centres of this Megacity once was in the borough of Brooklyn. Now it is in Manhattan. Living in New York City, for sometime, is highly educational for any foreigner. He confronts in his everyday work different types of people from different parts of America and also different parts of the world. He hears different accents of English language and becomes used to variations of accent. The presence of United Nations and the embassies of one hundred eight five countries of the world in Manhattan make it the most cosmopolitan amongst the cities of the world. One will come across these motley crowd speaking a medley of tongues in one's everyday life in New York city. We come across policemen in New York who may not be impressive as Americans because many of them may be foreign-born or native-born who have not given up their foreign accents. Chinese policemen are often seen in oriental neighbourhoods. So also Indian policemen in Flushing. Subway ride is an experience by itself, particularly in the rush hours of the day between seven and nine in the morning and five and seven in the evening. All the compartments are full with only a fraction of the people occupying seats, the rest remain standing with their hands clutching the hand rails over their heads, their bodies conforming to the contours of the persons infront or behind and their feet hardly touching floors. Very likely positions for crimes but hardly committed because of inability of persons to do so. You buy a token at the counter which will enable you to go to the platform. Using the token you can go as far as you want on the train. You could get down at any station you want to take another train for exchange at a suitable station or you can go to the entire length of the subway system without paying any extra cash. On Sundays and holidays art ful riders and visitors with appropriate guides can use this method to travel long distances by using a single token in the subways, In those days when I started in early 60's the price of one token was five cents. It has become almost two dollar now! Presently some computerised cards are being used for entry into the subway system and by using these magnetic cards at appropriate turn styles one can make the entry. The cards keep track of your subway trips and bill you through the credit card system at the end of the month. Living in New York city enables you to appreciate the role of automation, computerization, electronic signalling devices including telephone and automatic credit card systems for better utilization of advanced technology of the human society. If one technology is found suitable for applicability on a commercial basis, which can save one money and manpower, the same technology is used and adopted very quickly in the American society particularly in New York. Computers are everywhere in the world so also in New York city. Without computers very few organisations and equipment in the city can run. It seems almost all operations in big cities like New York are run by computers. No wonder the Headquarters of most of the computer companies IBM, AT&T, and other big giants are in New York city. They can not give up their base in New York city for anything in the world. All the automobile companies have headquarters in New York city. Since all these companies and businesses want to have their brains in New York city that adds to the importance of the city not only in respect of the economy of the US but in the economy of the world. Washington may be the political capital of America but New York is both political and commercial capital of the world. Nothing goes on in any part of the world without participation of New York in some area or aspect.

The Animal Medical Centre In New York City(A M C)

The new building of the Animal Medical Centre was commissioned in 1961. I joined the Institution in 1962, when everything at the Animal Medical Centre was in infancy. It was a six-storeyed building with only three floors functioning at the time of my joining. Enthusiastic participation of the employees in the developing programmes was typical from top to bottom. It appeared as if there was no limit to the monetary expenses at the institution. The Institution was possible by an original grant of six million dollars by the Caspary foundation, which made a bigger grant to the Rocke-feller Institute nearby. The members of the board of trustees usually competed with each other to grant donations and other funds for various programmes the Animal Medical Centre. However, the publicity associated with new and upcoming institutions created some animosity amongst the Veterinary professionals in the city and New York state including the Cornell University Veterinary College. The AMC was more affiliated to the Pennsylvania Veterinary college than with the Cornell University in its professional programmes. Two programmes at the AMC were conspicuous. One was the internship and residency programme for veterinary graduates; the second was research on comparative cardio vascular disease in animals. Since the AMC was having a clinical caseload of several thousand dogs and cats annually, along with a few other pet animals, this provided immense opportunity for study of heart disease in animals. University of Pennsylvania veterinary school was active in cardio vascular disease research at this time and thus was a appropriate partner in these programmes. Dr. Robert J. Tashjian who was the chief of staff of the AMC at the time was deeply involved in this study of heart disease in animals. He was collaborating with other scientists from University of Pennsylvania in this regard. He ultimately became the Director of the AMC in about a year. This facilitated orientation of the entire AMC to the study of heart diseae in animals. He was a very bright veterinarian trained in University of Pennsylvania, young and enthusiastic and perpetual bachelor. He was also a highly scholastic person and very knowledgeable. The project of study of heart disease in animals was sponsored by a large grant from the National Institute of Health which amounted to several million dollars over five year period. This grant was made possible by participation and recommendation by a famous cardio Vascular Scientist from University of Pennsylvania Veterinary College, Dr. David Detweiler, Professor at the Veterinary College. David Detwiler was a very famous name in Veterinary Cardiology. Because of his pioneering work at University of Pennsylvania in those days if Dr.

Detweiler recommended something it was approved at the National Institute of Health (NIH). The Animal Medical Centre benefited from this association. Dr. Detweiler's programme was enriched by his close association with the medical school of the University of Pennsylvania, which was next door.

Our programmes at the AMC on study of heart disease in animals was of a high standard, almost comparable to the similar projects on research on heart disease amongst the humans. The New York city had large number of Medical Institutions both colleges and hospitals, which had research programmes on heart disease because heart disease was a significant problem in human medicine. AMC's programmes were aimed at collaborating with many medical institutions in their heart disease programmes for its own benefit. We tried to copy as much as possible from some major medical school or hospitals to compare their studies with our study in animals. We found that there was a great deal of similarity in the study of pathology of heart disease in humans and animals. I took the initiative of having a few consultant Pathologists from the Medical Institutions regularly and participate in our study of pathology of animal disease, particularly the heart disease of animals. One of the major participants in this comparative study of heart disease was the Veterans hospital in the Bronx. This human hospital which had close to three thousand beds had a very big pathology department. The Chief and the associate Chief of the Pathology Department were happy collaborators at the AMC in our pathology programme. This improved the quality of work, we under took at the AMC. I also held a reciprocal position of consultant in pathology at the Veterans hospital in the Bronx. This association enabled me to further improve the quality of Pathology programme at the AMC.

Internship And Residency Programme at The AMC

In this programme we selected from all over the U.S.A. about twelve interns in various departments of Veterinary Medicine. After one year of internship they entered into a residency programme of about three years in six specialities. These specialities included a few sub-specialities in Medicine surgery and pathology. At the end of these three years of residency, these students appeared for a board certification by the American Veterinary Medical Association in respective speciality. This was a copy of the programmes in human medicine practised at the time. In Veterinary medicine this was one of the pioneering programmes in America. These few specialities of the earlier times have now expanded into about fifteen specialities in veterinary medicine. Now it is more elaborate in training and examination. The positions in various institutions in those specialities ask for people with board certification in these species or subspecies. So it has now become a very specialized work if one wants to teach or practice veterinary medicine in America in contrast to the olden days when a veterinarian used to practice all kinds of arts and science in Veterinary medicine. The AMC has continued these speciality programmes in large number of disciplines in small animal medicine where every year twelve to twenty specialists graduate from these programmes. Although the AMC is not a school or college, this programme of post-graduate training puts this institution on a high academic status at the level of postgraduate training programmes. Starting in early 1960. these programmes have produced hundreds of specialists in various branches of small animal medicine surgery and pathology. The staff of the AMC have produced many research and clinical publications in various aspects of small animal medicine. A few books have been compiled by authors from the AMC, Large number of people trained at the AMC have joined faculty positions in the various universities and veterinary schools. The research programmes oriented primarily towards clinical cases have enriched the literature of veterinary science in America. Within a few decades the AMC inspite of a few problems in administration and local pressures from the practising veterinarians has thrived and established itself on a solid foundation in the areas of small animal medicine and research. There is no denying that AMC has arrived.

I spent about ten years of my most active and productive life at the AMC. Because of the uncertainty of the new administration I decided in 1972 to relinquish my position as head of Pathology and Chief of staff. First I became the Director of the clinics of the humane society of New York for a year and then I established an animal hospital of my own, taking care of small animals primarily dogs and cats, but to have the availability of a second veterinarian I also bought a second animal hospital where I employed another veterinarian. The first two years of my independent ownership and management of animal hospitals I was quite comfortable. Suddenly there was a petroleam crisis in the world. Petroleum and its by-products became five or six times more expensive than the previous prices. This happened because of an oil embargo by the Arab countries, particularly against America. America was swimming in oil for its prolific economy. When oil was suddenly restricted American industry began to feel the pinch, like the fish in a drying pond. America after many tortuous maneuvres decided to accept very high price for petroleum and its products from the Arab world which was about six times the existing prices. This decision jolted American economy like we had never known. Oil is used to heat the homes in America in winters. Cars, trucks and all other machinery are fun on gasoline products. Ninety per cent of all activities in America are based on utilisation of petroleum products. America went into a sudden recession which would perhaps last for decades and longer. Animal hospitals which treated dogs and cats and other pet animals became victims of this recession in about a year. People became unemployed in large numbers. They had no spare money to have non- essential activities. So we Veterinarians who depend on the cash in the pockets of pet owners became victims. Many animal hospitals retrenched their programmes. I sold the second animal hospital quickly. I hung on to the first animal hospital although my income had gone down. As I did not have any better offer of employment, at that time I could not afford to be unemployed because my two sons were in the medical school.

Yonkers Animal Hospital

When I left the Animal Medical Centre for a new job, opportunities in New York city area appeared to be very small. The opportunities and the dimensions of the work I was conducting at the Animal Medical Centre was of a level of a top Veterinary College in the country and the clinical opportunities in New York City area could not be compared to that. Still I had to make compromise to accept the position of Director of Hospital at the Humane Society of New York, which basically was taking care of dogs and cats in large numbers. After working there for about a year I decided to have a hospital of my own if I had to depend on clinical treatment of animals for my livelihood. So, I decided to buy an animal hospital which was available for sale in Yonkers, New York. This hospital was a long existing one in the city of Yonkers at a distance of about twenty five miles to the north of Manhattan. It was a very busy practice of small animals primarily dogs and cats and kept one Veterinarian extremely busy. When I took over the hospital there was an English Veterinarian, Dr. Andrew Carmichael working full time in this place. After I bought the title to the hospital I asked Dr. Carmichael to continue for some time at least six months more to which he happily agreed. Dr. Carmichael was a graduate of Cambridge University, England and was experienced in American veterinary medicine for a few years at the AMC. In addition to Dr. Carmichael I used to work part time at this hospital. After Carmichael left I took over the practice all by myself. I used to have some surgeons from the AMC who would work part time with me. Dr. Greiner and Dr. Greene from the AMC were the two veterinarians who helped me at the Yonkers Animal Hospital on a part time basis. The first two or three years the Animal Hospital at Yonkers was very profitable for me. National economic recession as a result of the oil embargo affected the practice of the animal hospitals very adversely. Our incomes went down to less than half. A few Animal Hospitals closed down. Since this was the only source of my income I had to continue this operation till a suitable time when I could make a switchover to a more profitable enterprise. In 1981 I sold this animal hospital and accepted the position of Senior Veterinarian at the North Shore Animal League at Port Washington, Long Island which was about two miles from my home and very convenient for me. This new job also guaranteed higher income and other facilities to me. The Yonkers Animal Hospital where I used to see about fifty plus clinical cases of dogs and cats daily was a tremendous opportunity for clinical experience in small animals for me.

Sardar G.B. Singh, a retired Director of Veterinary Services of Orissa visited me for a few days when I was operating this animal hospital in Yonkers. Dr. Singh being a surgeon and very practical veterinarian was excited to see the operation of this animal hospital by me. I had the reputation of a pathologist, not a clinical Veterinarian, Dr. Singh was also professor of surgery at the Bihar Veterinary College while I was a student under him. After that we had joined the Orissa Veterinary Department. He was very complimentary to me seeing my adaptability to clinical practice being a pathologist and even expressed the desire to work with me in this animal hospital if it was physically possible for him. But this was only a statement, not a practical possibility because he was in his seventies and happily retired. I was very happy to have him as my guest for a while both at home and at the animal hospital where he used to spend part of the day with me.

The recession in American economy that affected my animal hospital business, lasted longer than ten years. But in the middle of the recession my sons graduated from the medical school and took up jobs in America, then I decided to sell the animal hospital and took on a salaried position with a local Veterinary Institution near my home with no loss of income. This was the job I took at the North Shore Animal League (NSAL). This was a position of clinical veterinarian which I occupied for about three years. It was very convenient to me because it was about two miles from my home.

North Shore Animal League (NSAL):

This was a non-profit Animal Hospital and adoption centre. It picks up stray animals from the street and maintains them and tries to adopt them out to private owners free. This organisation is a charitable one depending on the donations from public. This organisation collects amounts of millions of dollars a year. They employ about fifty people on their staff with aditional six to ten veterinarians to treat the sick animals. In general it can be called an animal centre with provisions for treatment and care of the sick animals they pick up. Although it began as a very small organisation, it had grown into its present form with aggressive management within last ten years. The standard of medical care was almost as good as any animal hospital but can not be compared to the academic standards of the AMC. The financial benefits to the employees was similar to those at the AMC. I spent about three years at this NSAL after which I left for a federal employment. There was a short period intervening between my leaving the NSAL and joining the Federal Govt. when I worked for an old friend of mine of the AMC who had instituted the AMC. He had established a small medical centre for animals in Boston area on the lines of the AMC of New York city. He wanted me to join there as chief of staff which I accepted. I had to commute from my home on the suburb of New York to Boston every week. I used to work there four days a week and return back on Friday. I was provided living quarters free of charge. The medical operation of this New England AMC of Dr. Tashjian was approachingly similar to those of the AMC at New York city. But the quality and the depth of the professional procedures of this new Institution were less extensive and also involved lesser number of clinical cases. The number of veterinarians involved was about five and other ancillary staff about ten. It was primarily a small animal hospital on a medium scale with more clinical work than research. However, there was a research project on a pernicious disease of horses called EIA, similar to AIDS in humans. The horses affected with this disease will Suffer from many years and waste away. The disease is caused by a virus like that of an AIDS virus. The horses had been transferred from the AMC's programme on EIA in New York city. These EIA positive horses were valuable researsch animals for comparative study of AIDS.

United States Government Service

During the middle of recession in America and towards the end of my tenure with the North Shore Animal League of Port Washington, New York, I had become a citizen of USA by call of circumstances. My daughter and her family visited us in 1983 for a prolonged period of about one year plus. It was found out that my daughter and her family had lost their permanent VISA status, because of overstay in India. To help them to get back their VISA status the only way was for me to apply for them as a citizen of America. I had lived in America for about thirty years by that time and qualified for being a citizen. So I applied for citizenship, and I got it in about a year. I actively looked for any opportunities in Federal Government as a Veterinary Pathologist, or as a supervisory Veterinarian. As usual with the Government it took several months before I accepted the position of a supervisory veterinarian in the North East region with headquarters in Syracuse. The regional headquarters was in Philadelphia. This region was responsible for the operation of meat and poultry inspection service in the states of North East in United States including Pennsylvania, New Jersey, New York, Connecticut, Vermont, Maine, Massachusetts, Rhode Island. My area included good part of New York, some part of New Jersey and some part of Vermont, Massachusetts and Maine. The job involved inspection and supervision of veterinarians and the inspectors employed in the meat and poultry plants in these areas. I being a trained Pathologist with a Ph.D. from Cornell University was considered as superior in qualification for this position. I had two supervisors, one as a Circuit supervisor and another as area supervisor. The area supervisor being a Cornell Graduate was very respectful to me. The inspectors who are non-veterinarians but trained in meat inspection by the veterinarians in the departments were supervised by me. These inspectors are usually college graduates with many years of training and experience in the department. They get practical training on meat and poultry inspection for about a year. These inspectors conduct animal by animal inspection or bird inspections on the lines of the Federal Government book on meat inspection. Their detailed procedures of inspection are supervised by me with any help and guidance in case of any problematic cases. Any case of animal or poultry where these non veterinarian inspectors have doubt are produced before me for further detailed inspection and disposal. Either the meat has to be passed for human consumption or rejected for destruction. We are guided by various short-period training courses and also a written manual of Federeal laws that passes or rejects such meat for human consumption. This Federal Manual not only insists on a uniform national standard but also has to take into consideration of international standards because many of these meat products are exported to many countries of the world. All these slaughter houses of meat and poultry have to maintain a uniform standard of cleanliness and sanitation and other operational proceedures ensuring clean and healthy meat production. The meat of these animals and birds have to be inspected by our staff to be free of disease conditions and abnormalities. These healthy and clean productions are guaranteed by enforcing a uniform code of inspection standards. These inspectors including the veterinarians that have jurisdiction over these plants are Federal Government employees where as the plants that conduct the slaughter and production of meat are all privately owned. They are usually huge operations individually, while some operations are very small dealing with few animals on a daily basis or a few hundred birds on a daily basis. The bigger operations involves Cattle, Sheep and Pigs. A big slaughter house on Pigs in my jurisdiction slaughtered about ten thousand animals a day. This may sound as a big operation in the North East region where I Worked. But some of the real big plants slaughter hundred thousand pigs a day. Compared to these Mid-Western slaughter houses the operations in the North East region are small. All slaughter house operations have to be inspected by the Federeal inspectors to ensure a uniform standard and health of the produced meat. Since, America depends on meat and poultry to a major extent for their daily diet, they allocate heavy funds to ensure the health and safety of the meat production system. However, production of meat and poultry is not conducted by the Government. These are privately operated. Many of these private operations or companies are huge and deal with millions and millions of birds and thousands of Cows, Swine and Sheep. Recently there is an emerging system of inspection of meat and poultry originating from wild animals and birds. Also there is a system of inspection of fish handled by bulk carriers and ships. America is famous for its mass production system. If they do not have a mass inspection system of these meat poultry and fish supplies, the public health will be in severe jeopardy. Americans are very conscious of that and therefore the Federal Government guarantees the health and safety of these food sources.

These concerns of the government for health and safety of the meat and fish supply has recently laid to impounding and arrest of some Indian owners of shrimp consignment originating from India. These businessmen were importing shrimp to America. By law these consignments of Shrimps must pass through sample checks of health and safety. But some of these samples, when tested, revealed pathogenic salmonela bacteria. Thus they were rejected. However, these Indian businessrien as usual in Indian circumstances took the ships' consignment to Scandinavian countries reprocessed and reached the shores of America again with the original supplies of shrimps Somehow these consignments were traced by the inspection authorities to the shrimps originally rejected calling for heavier penalties. The entire ship load of shrimps was condemned and destroyed and the owners and managers were imprisoned in federal prison for specified periods of time. The same level of penalizing jurisdiction is also available over the American business and companies involved in Meat and poultry industry. Once the department catches some parties committing these crimes the entire federal system comes down heavily on them.

Living in New York Area

Out of about forty years of my American experience I spent about thirty five years in or around New York city. I lived for about one and half years in Manhattan Island and about two years in Queens. After these initial years in New York city area! had a private home in Cambria Heights, Queens for about twelve years.

Home in Cambria Heights: This part of Queens is primarily a residential section having mostly single family homes. The homes ae beautiful, made of brick and stone with slate roof. Most of the homes are of colonial design. They were built in times of depression in America, during early 1930s, when labour and masons of Italian origin were cheaply available. Italian masons are famous for their quality of construction work. The house was located near the entrance to the state park way leading to Manhattan and opposite direction. There was a famous high school nearby so also several colleges and hospitals. The Kennedy International Air Port is about five miles from the area. When we moved to this house, my daughter had just been married in India and my two sons were going to high school in Forest Hills where we lived prior to Cambria Heights. My sons continued their school in Forest Hills because that high school was also reputed for quality education. This involved daily travel by my sons by bus and sub-way to cover a distance of about 10 miles one way. When we first moved in to this area of Cambria Heights, the population consisted of primarily Jewish and Italian people with very few blacks. Within a few years of our moving to this area there was a marked increase in black population. So much so that within about 10-12 years, the area became almost totally black. Along with the racial shift, crime and vandalism increased. The cleanliness and maintenance of homes began to show signs of neglect. The schools and other public institutions became affected with drug adiction and variety of crimes, Quality of education and other social programmes becans adversely affected Slowly and steadily there was a flight of better quality people from the area to other better localities, even though home prices were costlier in these better localities. My two sons completed their high school education while at this house. They were directly admitted to Manipal Medical College Mangalore in to their pre-medical course where they also completed their medical degrees. This house was centre of many social and cultural activities that my family organised or participated in. This house being located at the entrance to one of the major park (Cross Island Park) ways, was convinent for communication. We initiated and organised the Orissa Society At New York (OSANY) at this house. Many VIPs from Orissa and India visited us at this house. we had gatherings of Oriya community of New York and its vicinity regularly every month in this house. We observed many of our Indian functions and a few American functions here. The yearly feast of 'Thanks Giving Day' of the Oriya community was celebrated at this place. The children and new Oriya immigrants got a chance to get their feet on the ground with some degree of reassurance and reorientation in this new world, a world of plenty around them. We wanted to plant our Indian roots in this new land, called America and started to patronise Indian religious, cultural and social events. Our family actively participated in the new Hindu Temple being started in Flushing, New Yourk, with weekly Pujas on Sundays which was very welcome-occasion for mental peace and satisfaction in the new environment both for adults and children. This temple is now considered a masterpiece of Indian Temple Architecture in New York city. Cambria Heights brings to my mind many pleasant and sad memories, our first pet dog. named Rita, had lived with us in this house for about 12 years. Our second dog, named Bhalua, lived with us for about 10 years. Each of them was a valuable member of out family and very much loved. We cried for them individually when they died. My life and times at this Cambria Heights home epitomised my successes and failures in life in this new world. I am happy to say that the successes out-numbered the failures and I very fondly remember our days at Cambria Heights.

Thereafter I lived in a private home in Nassau County in Manhasset along with my children. This home in Nassau County was not more than twenty five miles from mid-town Manhatten. For two years I lived in a rented house, after which we bought the house next door. All the four children of my two sons were born in this house in Manhasset. I lived in this house with my two sons and their families for many years. My daughter and her family also visited us in this house for long periods. We have lived in this house for about sixteen years now. My elder son moved away to Wappinger falls up state New York about hundred miles from New York City, when he got his new job. He also bought a new house there. The house occupied in Manhasset was transferred to my younger son where my family has been living ever since. Long Island where we now live is the immediate suburb New York city to the east. Manhasset is a convenient town in Long Island within a radius of about twenty miles from Manhatten. It is an important name in Long Island, although it is a small town having about eight thousand homes. Large number of VIPs of New York city and New York State live in this town. There are several medical institutions in this area including the North Shore University Hospital. It is located in the North Shore of Long Island with a long shore line. It has a very regular fast train and bus connections with Manhattan. Schools are excellent. The School districts pay very top salaries to their teachers. Even the salaries of the policemen are in the top most range in America. Family incomes are hundred thousand dollars plus annualy. Home prices are very high, about half million dollars each. In short, this is a high quality, neat and clean, low crime town of highly educated people who are well employed. Doctors, lawyers, judges and well-known businessmen are amongst the residents. The shore lines of Manhasset has many picturesque and tourist attractions. It has also many good fishing places. The north shore of Long Island where Manhasset is located, is the home of many VIPs and famous families of New York. The bay connecting Manhasset with the Atlantic Ocean is a great area for sailing pleasure boats. There are thousands of them. The bay also provides great opportunity for fishing from the shore or from the boats. Although swimming facilities do exist in the waters of the north shore, this is not very good compared to the south shore. There are ample opportunity for shellfishing (Clams). Large number of people go for harvesting Clams in the shallow waters of the north shore. Sometimes these clams can be inedible when infected with Salmonella bacteria. This is detected by the health department of the state from time to time. If they detect presence of Salmonela, they publicize notices in the papers. Clamming is a fashionable picnic in America. Many families enjoy this picnic. Clams, oystsers and other kinds of Shell fish which are harvested from these waters are excellent for eating after baking or boiling. The north Manhasset bay extends north-east into the Atlantic Ocean with the rest of Long Island on its east side and state of Connecticut on the westside. This bay is used primarily by the pleasure boats and some tourist ships. There is no port for ocean liners because the water is shallow. Manhasset merges into another town on the north-east called Port Washington, which along with other towns of north shore are inhabited by the millionaires of New York area. So this north shore area is often named the "Gold Coast" in real estate literature. Many homes are worth millions of dollars with expansive acreages of land. These are the homes of people who are listed in V.I.P. lists of the New York metropolitan area. These people have no problem of earning money. They have problem in holding on to the profits and returns on their monies. If a millionaire has hundred million dollars, his annual income from the investments would run into tens of millions of dollars a year, without the consideration of salaries or other income. He or she is busy trying to retain as much of the profits and dividends on these tens of millions without paying it back to the federal government in taxes. So they retain high priced lawyers and accountants to do their paper work so that they pay the minimum tax possible. Since any charitable donations for causes like hospitals, educational institutions and other socially important institutions have this provision for tax deduction this is a big consideration in the minds of these rich people. They try to donate sizable amounts of money to various foundations and charitable institutions with the aim of controlling them. That is their objective. They get pleasure in controlling as many such charitable institution. This provision is guaranteed by the constitution and tax laws. New York metropolitan area is rife with people of this category, that is, rich and famous. Their worry is not to earn money but how to use the money they have to control and project their powers in the society. Many of the rich who are widows multiply their financial holdings by marrying wealthy widowers thus inheriting the estate after demise of their husbands, since women livelonger than men. There are not too many familar names in politics out of these overly rich people. Because most rich people do not like to join politics. It is only recently a few of the super rich have joined political positions. Usually they are behind important political personalities, whose view points they support. Most of these rich people are republicans and only small percentage of these super rich are democrats. American politics is primarily the struggle between the super rich and the ordinary people. The super rich people want to pay less taxes. So they can have more of their money to themselves. The ordinary people want the rich people to pay bigger taxes compared to the poorer. The political struggle and competition of the candidates in every two and four years are a reflection of this major view. During the post war era in America there is a trend where the richer segments are winning the race, by and large.

Socio Cultural Activities Of Indians

Indians including Oriyas are active in social and cultural forums in America which they have formed with their own funds for tax deductibility. Just like non-Government Organisations in India any nonprofit organisation and activity is subject to tax deduction that means anybody who donates any amount of money for this project gets the benefit from the income tax payable. Tax payment considerations are huge because almost everybody in America pays taxes which are calculated on higher rates for richer people than the people who have less. The socio-cultural endeavours include Churches, Temples. Schools, Colleges, Hospitals or other non profit activities are encouraged by these tax rules. Roughly a middle class person donating hundred dollars for such a cause saves fifty dollars on his tax bill. Hence this consideration is vital for the growth of such non profit institutions. Taking advantage of this provision many Indians and Oriyas likewise have created many non profit organisations. Large number of religious temples have grown up in America almost in each big city as a result of this consideration. The world famous ISCON grew out of this provision in taxes. One of the grandsons of Henry Ford donated a huge multi-storeyed building for ISCON. Many Indians have donated sizable sums of money to build temples which exist almost in every big city in America. The Hindu Temple Society of North America based on the Tirupati temple architecture has constructed a magnificent temple in New York City, for the worship of Shri Ganesh along with other Deities. I have personal knowledge of an anonymous donor giving a one time donation of 250 thousand dollars for this temple. I had the proud privilege of being associated with the board of trustees of this temple from the days of its foundation. This temple is a masterpiece of south Indian temple architecture and has also been listed and approved as a landmark building in New York city, which means it can not be demolished. Along with the regular daily worshipping of the deities in this temple, there is a huge auditorium on the land acquired next door for various cultural and social functions of the Indian community, like dance, drama and music. There are also educational programmes for the children of the Indian families in Indian religious and social customs. The temple also conducts free medical clinics and social counselling sessions for the Indian families. There are other programmes for the children and elderly Indians. The attendees are mostly Indian, although many Americans, white and black, attend these temples. C.V. Narasingham who was high in the command of the United Nations before long was the driving force and he was the founding president of this temple. There are about twenty other smaller temples in New York area. There is usually one or more Hindu temples in any medium sized city in America. In addition there are many other religious institutions like Gurudwaras and Mosques in America. All the mosques are founded by Arabian countries. The Orissa Society of America founded by Oriyas is active and functional in both America and Canada. They have branches in some of the major cities in America. The Orissa Society of New York (OSANY) which I had the privilege of founding became affiliated to the OSA in 1971, when the latter was founded. The OSA and Canada usually holds function once a year. While the affiliate local associations of which there may be ten or twelve, hold local cultural functions many times a year. OSANY was very active in its early days holding about six to eight functions a year in adition to collaborating with the parent organisation of the OSA in its annual function, OSANY's functions are usually cultural and religious mainly with ODISSI dances and music. Many dignitaries from Orissa and India were welcomed at special receptions. Many VIPs and culturally prominent individuals from Orissa were provided reception by the OSA at its annual functions. I had the privilege of receiving Hon'ble Satya Priya Mohanty, the ex-speaker of Orissa Legislative Assembly along with six other speakers in New York city when they were enroute to a conference of speakers to Canada. Other VIPS whom, I had the privilege of receiving in New York and entertaining in my home included ex-speaker of Indian Parliament Ravi Ray and his wife, Dr. Banshidhar Panda, Industrialist, Dr. Nimai Ch. Panda, ex-Director of health, Orissa, Hon'ble Rajendra Narayan Singh Deo, Chief Minister of Orissa, Hon'ble Surendra Nath Dwibedi, ex-Governor of Arunachal Pradesh, Mrs. Manorama Mahapatra, Associate Editor of 'The Samaj and her husband, now deceased, Padarabinda Mahapatra; Dr. Sitakanta Mohapatra (IAS) and Chamelli Mohapatra: Guru Kelu Ch. Mohapatra, Sri Raghunath Panigrahi, Sri Akhaya Mohanty, Sri Praffula Kar, Sri Pranab Pattnaik. Mrs. Sanjukta Panigrahi, Sri Gangadhar Pradhan and others. The OSA Indians in America particularly in New York had busy schedule over the weekends and other vacation days participating in Indian functions, either in our linguistic social groups or other Indian groups. Columbia University had an active Indian organisation and had regular programmes in social and cultural areas. They also celebrated the Indian religious festivals particularly the Durge Puja which was conducted in a tremendous scale at Columbia.

Mr. Saradendu Mishra son of late Shyam Sundar Mishra and his wife Lata Mishra presented weekly Oriya music programme through Columbia University Radio, The Oriya group in New York had several annual programmes on a regular basis. They had picnics, swimming trips in the beaches of New York and New Jersy, a camping trip in south Jersy or Pennsylvania (POCONOS) and once in up state New York.

Blooming Burg Farm Picnic

I had a farm of about thirty six acres with some fruit

trees, grapes, cherries in Middle Town, New York that is where our group of OSANY gathered for one day trip. About twenty to twenty five Oriya families, members of OSANY gathered at this place. We had some light lunch followed by heavy dinner cooked outdoors at this farm. Menus included rice dal, vegetable curry, goat meat curry and other dishes. There was a cultural afternoon of music and walking in the woods with picking of apples, berries and cherries. Some of the members overnighted at the farm till late next day. This place was about sixty miles north west of New York city & located in a beautiful semi rural, hilly area. In America such areas with hills, valleys & woods with nearby streams are ideal for picnic sites & group gatherings in the summer & fall. Particularly if these places are within hundred miles radius of big cities they are ideal spots for such outings. This small farm was set on the side of a picturesque hill, With all kinds of wild fruit trees & cherries there were lots of deer in the woods. You can see them in the backyard and crossing the road inside the farm & also when you are leaving the farm. They had no fear at all. Because nobody can shoot them except during the hunting season. When you get up early in the morning you see dozens of these huge deer happily grazing in your vegetable yard. It was a great enjoyment to watch these beautiful animals at such close quarters although they were having breakfast of our garden. Prior to this place in middle town I had a bigger farm in Oneonta in up state New York.

Oneonta Farm

This farm was about hundred fifty acres in size & located about 175 miles from New York city. This farm also was primarily a hobby farm. It had about fifty acres of woods, ten acres of apple orchard, two animal sheds, a pond & riding area of about ten acres. We had lot of enjoyment at this farm over the weekends. When my children first arrived at New York, I had the occasion to buy this farm. We kept this farm for about two years but we sold it when my family became smaller after my daughter got married. Although I had been in this town of Oneonta for about two years, I developed many friends amongst the Americans in this area, who were very helpful to me. After my daughters marriage to Ranjit Kr. Mohanty the eldest son of Industrialist Naba Kishore Mohanty of Jhanjhimangala, Cuttack, we moved back to New York city area for continuation of childrens' education etc.

In this rural area of Oneonta I developed some good friends amongst the American families. One was Frank Reeves. He was a lawyer and took care of my legal matters. He was a great personal friend and would give all kinds of help legal or private. He was an affectionate man and loved my family & children very much. He was very sad to see my daughter Dolly getting married at such a young age of sixteen whom he loved very much as one of his children. However, when I needed some monetary help from the Bank in connection with my daughters marriage, he used his influence and acquaintance with the Bank's Vice President to grant me a loan of 5,000 dollars on a nominal mortgage of my newly acquired land in Oneonta. He also stood as a personal surety for the loan. He was a typical large-hearted American. We became very good family friends and whenever I needed some help, I would call on him or his wife and the help would be forthcoming. Taxes of this farm used to be very low about 2 or 3 hundred dollars a year, but I had a contract with an Oil Company which would pay this tax with the provision that any Oil exploration right in my property would first be given to them. So I need not have to pay taxes at all. There is a permitted hunting season for deer usually in the months of November and December. Since I had about fifty acres of woods in my property which had deer; many hunters would come to me with gifts of wine and whisky etc. for the privilege of hunting in my property. There were lot of mature lumber in the property; people come to buy this for cash. Some folks would request one or two trees for lumber. I would give them free of charge. During the rest of the year that is except November and December no hunting of deer is allowed in the region. One can still hunt small games like rabbits at other times of the year. My children adopted a rabbit, named Harvey and made a run with wire netting of about twenty feet square. The wire netting was dug deep about two feet below the ground to prevent him from going out. However very often he would escape through the holes, dug deep under the ground and would sit outside the enclosure.

We had bought a horse for riding for children. It cost two hundred dollars. It was an American saddle horse. It was big and beautiful. It spent major part of the day under the apple trees eating fallen apples. Sometimes it would suffer from indigestion. Her name was Diny. She gave us a foal whose name was Cheyenne, named after an American Indian tribe. Both were often times under the apple trees eating the fallen apples. They had a grazing area of about five acres plus. They spend the whole day outdoors and come to the Verandah in the evening. There was a big trough of water outside. They are given some grains of horse feed at night to bring them in. Diny was a nice riding horse. I and my children used her for riding in the farm. My elder son Akhaya was incharge of the horses. My daughter Dolly was incharge of the bull calf named Michael and my younger son Annada was incharge of the chicken that numbered about twelve. The farm next door had the privilege of cutting the hay from my farm and take half and leave half for the animals. In the summer time both of my sons who were going to high school at that time used to work with this farmer. They used to spend the whole day with him taking care of the cows and working in the fields for free lunch and about fifty dollars a month each. Monetary benefit was small but it trained my young sons in hard work in American farm life, which would be very useful in their future in America. On the weekends my whole family would go out to the parks for picnicking and fishing. There were a few good picnic spots near the local lakes. There were also excellent fishing spots in these lakes and in the river which flowed through this town. We were very happy when we lived in this area, because the local people were very receptive and kind to us. In addition to that summer time was full of bounty of crops, vegetables and fruits in this area. Being a small town things were very cheap compared to New York. We used to locate some goats in some farms and get them slaughtered at the local slaughter houses. They would pack them into smaller packets ready for the freezer. We had a freezer which would hold thousand pounds of meat and fish. Whenever I used to find some cheap meat or fish I would buy them and put them in the freezer. Most of the time, our milk supply was from our neighbor farmers, who delivered five gallons of milk daily. It was very cheap compared to the rates in the stores. We used to grow corn (maize), Cucumbers, egg plants (brinjal), tomatoes, green peepers and some squash in our farm. Other vegetables we used to buy from outside. There were plenty of apples for a good part of the year. The only thing we needed to carry from New York were Indian grocery and spices. Many Indian and American friends visited us during the summer time in this farm, so also many Oriyas. Many young veterinarians & paramedics from the AMC would visit us at this farm on weekends and short vacations. Once a group of interns and some nursing staff of the AMC made an overnight camp in the hay stack of one of our barns: Several German veterinarians who were on the junior staff at the AMC also visited us for picnicking & riding. Our horse Diny was a good sport for such occasions. In summer time also we made many trips from the farm to thousand Island Area which is on the borders of the U.S.A. and Canada. This is a very picturesque area where there are about seventeen hundred Islands in St. Lawrence River, separating US.A. and Canada. Fishing opportunities are abundant, so also for swimming and boating. During the summer time this area on the nothern part of New York State is a vacation paradise. This is located in an area of the state which is owned by New York state parks department and available for public use. There were hundreds of cabins provided with electricity and refrigerator and two or four beds, which can be occupied during the non-winter months. The fee for these cabins for a week is about fifty dollars. These have cooking facilities on the outdoor grill. Swimming and boating and fishing are free. You have your own boats or you can rent some boats locally. Opportunities for fishing in this area is one of the best in the world. Either you can fish from the shores or from the boats. The St. Lawrence river is very deep. At some spots it is four hundred feet deep. In the winter months the surface freezes, but water flows below. So St. Lawrence river is rich in all kinds of fresh water fish. Opportunities for pleasure boating is tremendous. Therefore, during the summer time this area is full of tourists and vacationers. One can cross the river over a huge bridge connecting Canada.

Canadian Trip Via Thousand Island Bridge

One can visit Canada by crossing the Thousand Island Bridge to the otherside of the river. At the middle of the bridge there is a mark noting the boundary of U.S.A. & Canada. Within a few feet of this international boundary on each side there is the immigration office of each country. If you are entering Canada you have to show your passports & other papers to Canadian immigration office & Canadians & other visitors from the opposite side will have to show their passports & other papers to the U.S. immigration office. If you are a permanent resident of either country you may have either the Passport or the green card. These documents will allow free entrance to either country. If you are a visitor from other countries like India, you have to have authorized VISA for entry into Canada or U.S.A. respectively. For Indian passport holders who want to visit Canada or America have to write to the appropriate immigration office for VISA ahead of time. Once cleared at the border one is free to travel inside Canada wherever one wants to go. For about hundred miles from the border with the U.S. Canadian countryside appears similar to that of the U.S.A. with the decreasing traffic as you go north. The cities & the towns within about hundred miles of the border are similar to American counterparts. But after about hundred miles the population in Canadian countryside becomes sparse and the houses also appear different and less prosperous. The traffic is much less on the road. There are fewer rest areas. The trees and forests appear to be less luxuriant. There are fewer villages and towns on the roadside. The few farms with grazing Holstein cattle appear to be less prosperous than the U.S. counterparts. The inter connecting roads are fewer & fewer as you drive north. One gets the impression of abrupt end to the population centres of Canada which appear to be located near the bordering regions of the United States. However, once you enter into the cities like Montreal,or Toronto, you feel you are inside a prosperous American city. The Canadian cities particularly Montreal are very clean and organized. Although the traffic inside the cities appear to be markedly less. The roadside facilities for parking and other amenities are fewer compared to the American side. The local people are very pleasant and cooperative to provide services to the American visitors. Food prices in the restaurants are cheaper by American dollar. The Canadian Dollar is about 85 cents of American currency. Canadian people appear to be very helpful and cooperative to American guests. They welcome you with open arms. One visit of our whole family during a camping trip to the Algon Quin National park in the state of Ontario was not very impressive, with regard to basic sanitation and other amenities. There are large number of Indians particularly Sikhs in many parts of Ontario state particularly in the city of Toronto. These people are quite prosperous as professionals and businessmen. Many Indians hold high elective offices and are employed in the govt. jobs in good numbers. The city of Toronto appears to be less populous and more organized compared to the American counterparts. The overall picture of Canada after one leaves about fifty miles from the international boundary with U.S.A. is one of the low population. The canada has only 23 million people as compared to about 240 millions of United States. Canada is a huge country and is in the need of further industrialization and exploitation. Its immense landmass with unlimited natural resources of gasoline and variety of minerals has offered a constant invitation to the world's immigrants. Indians should open their eyes to Canadian immigration. Canada particularly wants Indian immigrants who are scientifically and technologically educated. Lot of Canadians also cross over to the American side and vice versa. About hundred miles to the West of Thousand Island is one of the world's best fishing spots for Salmon fishing, This is the mouth of the Oswego river. This river falls into the big lake Ontario. In the month of September and October, if you go with fishing rod and tackle, you can catch salmon fish as long as 5-6 feet weighing hundreds of pounds. You are allowed to only catch one per head. This is the area where the salmons come upstream from the lakes to spawn. They go up the river, upstream even jumping over barriers of bridges and embankments. They come by the thousands from the lake upstream during this part of the year. In fishing line thrown at them they would swallow and try to run away with the line, sinker and the rod. One has to have a long reserve spool of fishing line in hundreds of feet of lengths, because the fish is going to carry the line into the lake. If you are lucky you catch one Salmon in the whole day after losing twenty or thirty such big fish in the line. Thousands of people from all over the world particularly from U.S.A. come for fishing in these parts. Each is allowed to only carry one salmon; may be fifty to two hundred pounds in the weight.

    Living in New York or in America is very enjoyable if you can make some time daily or weekly or monthly outside your required routine of the job. There is so much of the outdoors and indoor activities for you to enjoy. In America most people would retire earlier than later than their retirement age and enjoy the beauty and bounty of the country that it is. America is full of woods and prairies in most of the area. They want to keep the country that way filled with natural beauty. Since, there is plenty of land left for agriculture & other enterprises apart from these reserved areas, instead of acquiring lands from the wild areas they go on buying up adjacent private lands to make the state parks bigger & more enjoyable by the public. In New York State alone one major state park named Adirondaks in the north of the state measures about six millions acres, which is expanding from time to time. These parks are available for recreation & sports facilities for the public both in the New York State and outside New York state. There is a small fee for use of many man made facilities in this park. During the summer time these parks are heaven for vacationers who can rent cabins with cooking facilities for five dollars a day or they have their own tents. They can rent a space for camping for one or two dollars a week. There are public bathrooms and toilets in the area for use for free. You can fish on shore as much as you want. Most families catch enough fish for their day's use. Cooking needs by American families are limited because of their eating habit. If they have bread, milk, fruits and some meat or fish that is enough for their needs. By Indian standards American eating habits are simple but nutritious. Since summer time is busy for vacationing, one has to make reservations in these parks ahead of time. This can be done by telephone through a central office for all the parks in New York State. People usually spend one or two weeks at a time in these parks. Camping is most inexpensive and enjoyable for the entire family. In one of these camps my younger son would spend hours chasing some huge carps with his fishing tackle. If you don't have the right bait, then they won't bite. Most of the time we catch, lots of fish to carry back to our home after the vacation is over. Usually we fry them in the open fire outside the cabins before we carry them home. We can keep them in the freezer for the future use long after the vacations.

Florida Trip

Among many short or long trips to Florida I conducted one major trip that included my whole family. When the children were in schoolgoing age we visited many places in the Eastern United States and also were guests with many Indian and American families along the route to Florida. This trip was an enchanting sight seeing trip for all of us, particularly for my children who were visiting Florida for the first time. Florida is derived from the word "Flower" and is every bit beautiful suggestive by its name. It is decorated by nature by green trees with permanent bloom of various flowers along the route. The luxuriant growth of wild flowers along the highways presented the garlands of welcome to the incoming visitors with gorgeous welcoming sign. There were orchards of various kinds of fruits along the route, specially the groves of orange, lime and tanzarines. These fruits in various stages of ripening present a beauty out of this world. Along the route we visited some American Indian communities which was a stark example of poverty and neglect compared to the regular American countryside. This can be a rude reminder of disparity of development of various communities in America. But it must be appreciated that

American Indian communities are responsible for their own situation. Because they choose to remain in self-imposed isolation in their own independent areas outside the constitutional United States. The Constitution of United States guarantees the freedom of these indigenous People of America and their ways of life.

Florida is endowed with a huge coastline on the east coast and also in the west coast of the peninsula which provides swimming and fishing facilities along with all kinds of water sports. The natural beauty of the peninsula Florida with its green foliage and aquatic life is a beauty to behold. Since there is no snow in the winter time and weather is around seventy degree Fahrenheit most of the winter American tourists from the mainland flock to Florida. There is a huge tourist industry in Florida. Disney World has made special attractions for visitors to Florida. This creation of artificial panorama in the setting of Florida which is already beautiful by its natural beauty has added tremendous attractions for all kinds of tourists to this area which is located in the middle part of florida away from the coast. In America driving on long trips in the countryside is a pleasure by itself. New visitors to the country on these driving trips are impressed by the natural and artificial decorations on the roadside with welcoming signs for the tourists. All these roads have access to very good restaurants along with parking lots along the way for the relaxation of the tourists. And you end your travel by car at the tip of the land mass of America in Florida. They have still created roadways through the waters of the Florida bay towards, Cuban Island. One can drive about ninety miles on the highway to the deeps of these chains of Islands known as key west. From key west to Cuba it is only about 90 miles by water. There is no road connection connecting the American main-land with Cuba, Most visitors ride to the tip of the key west and return to the main-land. We did the same. Both while driving to and from key west Florida towards the main land we had ample places for our road side picnics and lunch. Red snapper was a special fish delicacy to enjoy during our trips.

Hunting

Hunting is a very common pas-time for Americans. They hunt all kinds of animals in woods most of the year. Most Americans have guns, except where restricted by laws. Americans have a Constitutional right to possess guns. So roughly more than half of American families have some guns. They can hunt not only for large animals like deer and bear. They also hunt for rabbits and other small game animals in their spare time. Since most of America has woods nearby and people have cars, they use these hunting facilities very frequently. There are extensive laws and regulations to control the hunting activity, particularly for hunting deer. There is restricted period of the year when you can hunt for deer usually about a month before the freezing weather of November and December. There are also detailed rules, what kind of deer one can hunt and how many one can take. Usually one hunter can take one deer only, and these have to be of certain age which are determined by size of his horns. Recently because of population explosion by the deer, some areas in America, particularly in New York State it has been allowed to sell deer meat commercially. Otherwise this was prohibited by law before. In some deep woods, there are also breeding bear. These can also be hunted under such some restrictions. Some people eat bear meat. There is almost no restriction for hunting of small games like rabbit, squirrel etc. There are no wild animals like tigers and lions in the woods in America. At best for as much there may be small mountain lions in same parts of America, which are allowed to be hunted. Otherwise most of the woods are free of dangerous wild animals. Most of the time the woods are free of poisonous snakes, except in some areas where there are large number of rattle snakes. In the woods where rattle snakes are known to be living it is usually marked out with warning signs. Most Americans know how to hunt rattle snakes. In some regions where rattle snakes are common, the local people eat then. In Texas there is a period of the year where they have a festival of eating fried rattle snakes. I have seen some rural towns, south of Dallas, Texas where there were common places with pits for boiling rattle snakes in oil. During a particular period of the year when they know rattle snakes are in large numbers, local people would catch them by the dozen. They usually cut their heads and tail off before frying. It is said that rattle snake meat is good to eat like that of fish. At least this is a way to control the population of rattle snakes in the area.

Public Entertainment And Sight Seeing Opportunies In New York City

New York city is known as the entertainment capital of the world. New York city has all kinds of entertainment going on almost everyday in the year. There are innurnerable sight seeing events in this area. Many cultural and entertainment centres are located in the city where they present programmes on various subjects. Theatre in English language are presented in many halls almost on a continuing basis throughout the year. Some individual theatre programmes have continued for years together. Hundreds of folks provide programmes of dance, drama and music throughout the city almost on a continuing basis. Amongst the English speaking world New York will be the top in theatre and entertainment area. Most of the renowned artists are active in New York city. The talent is par excellence and audience is sophisticated enough to pay the high prices of these performances. Many of the audience make reservations a year ahead of time and make inter continental flights for the purpose. Special programmes presented by artists from various countries are always common. Modern American dances are also part of these programmes. There are enormous galleries, exhibition halls and other public places of interest in New York city, where one can spend days browsing. People can also get free tickets to participate in the live telecasts of different television stations which are located in New York city. There are guided tours by bus and by ships of the city and its surroundings. There are thousands of people employed in the sight seeing tours to show the city around to the visitors. There are so many things to see and do in New York in the entertainment area that one can spend months visiting various parts and activities of New York on a full time basis. People come from all over the world to see the activities of New York. They spend more than half of their time just watching New York city, watching New York city buildings, sky scrapers, roads, highway, tunnels, without having gone inside one of the buildings. When one enters into one of the buildings like United Nations or any one of the Galleries, he can not end seeing all these in one day. In that area New York city is a unique centre of human activities unparalleled in the world. One does not realise what he is missing if he has not been to New York city. New

York city appears to be a permanent exhibition ground for the sightseer.

Sea Food Market In New York City

New York city is one of the major markets of sea food. Everyday before down shiploads and truck loads of sea food arrive in New York from all over the world, particularly from the waters in and around America. One of the major markets on the East Coast of America is at Fulton street of Manhattan Island and also South side of Bronx known as hunters point market. These markets only sell sea foods on a wholesale basis. Although some retailers have shops nearby. If one is ambitious to buy wholesale he can buy this sea food at very small prices. You have to clean and process them yourself. Cleaning and cutting the fish is an extra burden one has to consider while buying wholesale. The cost of fish and other sea food in these markets can be 1/3 the price of the same in retail shops. There are also many retail fish stores which are in between the wholesale and retail. Such stores buy fish and other sea food in bulk from the Fulton Street and hold them in their room size freezers. If you buy fish in bulk from these stores they can cut and clean your fish for a small fee. But their basic price is much lower than regular retail stores. Since thess big stores charge lower prices for bulk buyers, I used to buy variety of fish about hundred pounds at a time and have them cleaned there. We store these in our freezer at home. In New York area we used to enjoy fish more than meat. One can get all kinds of fish in New York area both from fresh water and salt water. Carp (rohu) and Buffalo Carp (Katla or Vakur) are available in plenty. They originate from the fresh waters of the rivers and lakes. Some of the common salt water fish which we like are weak fish, Blue fish, Mackerel, Butter fish and Porgies. Ilisa (Shad) is not preferred because of its bones, but available in plenty in season. Shrimps of all sizes are available from the local waters or from imports from other countries, particularly South America. Hotels and Restaurants order their own fish supply through the wholesalers. This fish are usually large fish which can be sliced into steaks and boneless. Such fish can be salmon and all other kinds of Sea fish which are big in size. Fish roe of various types are imported to New York harbor. The roe of the big sturgeon which are of the size of small grapes are imported at very fancy prices. Many other speciality meats of marine sources are also available in New York area. Some of the gourmet shops in New York can procure for you any kind of fish or marine meat if you order either from inland sources or from abroad.

Long Island Beaches

New York is blessed with extensive Ocean beaches in Long Island, particularly in the South shore, extending about 150 miles from the Manhattan Island. These beaches offer best facilities for swimming, camping, fishing and boating. Thank God most of the beaches are not owned by individual public, but by state and the National Governments. The huge waves of the Atlantic Ocean hit these beaches continuously. Majority of the beaches are shallow and fit for swimming. Rarely there is shark infestation in any of the beaches. In spite of publication in a book about the killer shark, there has been no such instance in the Lang Island beaches. These books were fiction. Since a good part of this long beach is owned and operated by the Federal Government, they offer an excellent setting for camping and other activities. There are extensive areas reserved for parking of cars adjacent to each beach. There are facilities for bathrooms and dining in the Central building. Next to the parking lots there are tens of miles of board walk facing the Ocean. Between the board walk and the waters are extensive sandy beaches which may be half a mile wide throughout the length. Swimming is promoted in the entire beach area and a few life guards are in attendance most of the time during summer months. The beaches are patrolled by the U.S. Coast Guards in medium sized steamers who may come to the rescue of any swimmer needing help. The best time for of enjoying the beaches is the summer and part of the fall. Of many beaches I have visited in America, Long Island beaches on the South shore can come in the first category of the American beaches. Going to the beach is usually a full day programme. One carries barbecue supplies and drinks. No alcoholic beverages are allowed on the public beaches. One can swim in the most of the beaches, Fishing is allowed in majority of areas. Affinity groups can have their many functions in some parts of the beaches without any problem. Long Island beaches can be best enjoyed on bright sunny days from end of May through September. Although many hardy people enjoy the beaches in cooler days through December. There are great fishing opportunities throughout the 150 miles of the beaches. There are fishing boats which go into the deeper waters of ocean from five to ten miles of the coast for selective fishing by angling. The boat management knows the favourite fishing spots and takes the passengers there for a satisfactory day for fishing. One can fish for Bass, Blue fishs, Porgies and Flukes. Selectively in many areas, going in boats for a whole day trip is a great pleasure and is profitable to comeback with a load of fish at the end of the days and it costs you only ten dollars. Many people have their many small and medium boats for family fishing. Fishing in ones own boat is more risky off the coast of Long Island. Particularly in bad weather one has to be careful. But you are safe in bigger rental boats where the operators are more knowledgeable about the weather conditions and particular areas of the waters. You have to realise that you are in the Atlantic Ocean.

Maine Lobster

Lobsters are like huge Shrimps with distinctly large claws. These are great delicacies of food in many parts of the world. America is specially rich in this breed of crustacean, particularly in the northern climates. In the coast of Maine these Lobsters are harvested in great quantities. They are also caught in moderate numbers in lower latitudes as far as New York. The coast of Maine is famous in the East Coast for these Lobsters. They are one to ten pounds in average size. They can be enjoyed like Shrimps. First they are boiled in water for about twenty minutes. Usually the heads are separated and handled in separate way. The good part of the meat is in the rest of the Lobster which is called the tail. After removing these shells the body is full of meat. These can be one and half feet long and few inches in diameter. On the back of this meaty part of the body there is a streak of gray which is the intestine. These intestines can be removed by splitting the Lobster backs very often. One does not have to resort to this delicate carving procedure. The meaty body of this Lobster called the tail can be enjoyed in many different ways. A typical American Lobster dinner comes with a cup full of melted butter of several ounces. And one is supposed to dip pieces of this Lobster meat in this butter and eat. Although it is delicious to have Lobster meat in this way, this type of meal is supersaturated with cholesterol and may not be scientific or very healthy. But many Americans who enjoy food never give any attention to the health effects of such food. Lobster heads can be cooked separately, although in most American restaurants they are never served except as soup. We have enjoyed the Lobster heads cooked after boiling as usual and they are delicious. They can be cooked as curries with potato, onions and tomatoes and can be great delicacy as Indian Lobster curry. There is usually plenty of meat inside these shells of the head of the Lobster. While driving in the coast of Maine particularly around Portland, a sea port in Maine, one can enjoy very inexpensive lunch and dinner with Lobster ranging from five to ten dollars. These Maine Lobster are shipped to almost all over the United States by parcel post for overnight delivery. Most of the big cities have fresh Lobster for sale in the fish department of many high quality food shops. I had the privilege of an assignment in Maine while under the appointment with the Federal Government. I enjoyed these Lobster dinners along with my family and appreciated God's special kindness to America in providing food ad libidum in every area you look. While travelling in the southern parts of America in the state of Maryland and Virginia again under Federal Government assignment, we also enjoyed local harvest of blue crabs for dinner. It is another enjoyable delicacy like the Maine Lobster. These Crabs are available in the coastal waters of the Atlantic Sea board, specially at the mouths of big rivers around the Chesapic bay. These Crabs are about four to five inches long and three inches diameter and boiled in salt water with mild spices. There is a special way how to handle them and eat them with small forks.

One can eat may be six to twelve crabs at a time. They are great delicacies to have in lunch or dinner. Some would only have crab for dinner with some Salad, others may have some bread and butter along with them. We enjoyed with salad. Again a full meal with a dozen boiled blue crabs and all other accessories is about ten dollars a dinner, which can be more expensive if it is farther from the coast. While driving in America one gets constantly impressed as to the richness and variety of food supply throughout the country. Not only they harvest agricultural crops, fruits and vegetable grown on land more than plenty in America, but also the food derived from the animals and marine sources are equally plentiful. One wonders how the Lord was extremely partial to Americans in creating this bounty for them and around them, although the Americans themselves have contributed greatly to this surplus by their own productivity and preservation.

"Thanks Giving Day"

There is an Annual Festival in America for "Thanks Giving Day". This is celebrated all over America to offer thanks to Almighty God for the blessing of plenty to the American people. This is celebrated on the fourth Thursday of November every year. Historically it goes back to the days of the pioneers who had the first harvest of crops in the American soil in the New England area. They celebrated it with plenty of foods from their own lands and the meat of wild turkeys. This festival and memories are celebrated throughout America with food in plenty. The ceremonial meat which is the staple American food on this occasion is from these turkeys which are specially slaughtered in millions. The present day turkeys are quite different from the wild turkeys. The Americans hunted these Turkeys in their early days for celebration of Thanks Giving. The present day turkeys are specially bred to be meaty and huge and weigh upto about fifty pounds individually. Usually the biggest turkey in the country is presented to the White House by the breeder. We Oriyas used to celebrate this Thanks Giving day with great excitement. It is a nonreligious festival observed by all Americans. We celebrate the blessings of plenty by the Almighty. Usually my house was the centre of this celebration where all the local Oriyas joined together for the Thanks giving barbecue turkey. By this method the whole turkey is cooked inside a gas or electric oven for three to five hours at a certain temperature. It has to be wrapped in aluminium foil before cooking. It is tested frequently as to the tenderness of the meat by piercing testing hooks in the meat. If it is well-done the hooks go in easily. If it is not it will require a little bit more cooking. There is also a special thermometer which pops out of the turkey when it is well-done. Depending on the size of the turkey it needs about three to five hours Oven time at a particular temperature. In the early days we used to have only one 22-pound turkey for the group. Later on when the group became bigger we used to have two such. There are some other ancillary dishes which are to be prepared for completion of the MENU of turkey. One is a gravy mixed with the juice of the turkey. Two, stuffing consisting of mixed vegetables, bread crumbs, Onions etc. and spices. Three, Blue Berry pie. Many of the adult members of the group also enjoy varying amounts of alcohol as long as they are indoors. Since the festival is during the last week of November which is a cold month in New York, nobody feels like being outdoors for any length of time. Turkey day is a national holiday in America and is enjoyed by all. We immigrants happily enjoyed this day with sumptuous quantity of food and fun. I remember it was a great source of excitement and pleasure for us, the immigrant Oriya community, to be a part of this function in America which was not restricted to any particular religion. I thought it was a real national festival and fit for American affluent spirits. I enjoy almost every year a ceremonial turkey dinner either at my home or in the homes of some of my close American friends. The Oriyas who enjoyed the turkey dinner most were the second generation Oriyas like my grand children. These children of school and college going age are not very fond of Indian food dishes. They do not like spices and some would not like the over seasoned Indian method of cooking. They enjoy chunks of meat in their dinner not like the side dishes of meat or fish served in Indian fashion. They enjoy meat as their staple food. On Thanksgiving Day these children relish the turkey dinner to their utmost satisfaction. They can have as much turkey meat as they need without spices or seasoning. This non-spiced turkey meat may sound to Indian ears not very appetizing but one has to have practical participation to appreciate the enjoyment. No wonder the second generation of Indian children are growing healthier and bigger than their parents.

Barbecue Chicken And July Fourth

Another ceremonial dish we used to enjoy was a most common American delicacy made out of chicken called barbecue chicken. This is a whole chicken or split chicken cooked in the open fire in a special but simple process called "Barbecue". Basically it is a big piece of chicken or meat baked in open fire. This custom is derived from the common habits of the 'American Indians who used to cook their meat this way. At present various seasonings have been developed to wet the chiken with a hand brush with these spicy and oily mixtures while the chicken is being cooked. It has a special taste and appeal to the entire family when this is cooked outdoor's in the backyard. Other assortment of dishes may be cooked to go with barbecue chicken but a salad including cucumber, tomatoes, lettuce, sliced green pepper with a little bit of salad dressing is a good combination. Most American families will have a few corn on the cob along with chicken barbeque. This is a common family programme to have chicken barbeque in the backyard on the weekends and brief holidays. July 4th is celebrated with great pomp and splendour of over America with an occasion to enjoy chicken barbeque in the backyard with friends and relatives. July 4th is the day America got its independence from the British and adopted the new constitution. It is a great national holiday observed with fanfare throughout the country. New York areaobserves it with great fireworks and many sailing ships at the mouth of New York harbour. July 4th can be called the greatest national holiday in America.

Miscellaneous American Food Items

America provides opportunity for all ethnic groups of the world to present their speciality food items in the American markets. Such items are innumerable and can include Peking Ducks, Sturgeon's Caviar, Beef Goulash etc. There are many palatable dishes made of meat, chiken and shrimps by Italian chefs which are very tasty, but expensive. Recently some of the Indian dishes of meat and fish have been introduced in America which are also liked.

Tandoori chicken is one of the Indian dishes one likes in America, so also Nan and mutton curry with less spices New York city is a gourmet's paradise where delicacies from each of the countries of the world are available as lunch or dinner menu. In Manhattan these exotic dishes are served inexpensively in hundreds of these restaurants, all priced under ten dollars. If one likes to go for the most common American lunch menu, sausage and meat balls at lunch time in Manhattan Island he can pay less than five dollars, with free supply of bread, butter and cold drink. In our early days in Manhattan I used to have a big hero sandwich for lunch weighing about one and half pounds for one dollar twenty five cents. The same might have become five dollars now. Manhattan is not only the capital of Art, learning and business, it is also the capital of the world as regards the luncheonettes and restaurants. Along with the privilege of unlimited sight seeing a visitor to Manhattan has unique opportunity in sampling all kinds of international dishes at a very inexpensive price. If one wants the cheapest lunch at noon time one can get a sandwich from the many push cart vendors on the roadside consisting of variety of meats and chicken and lots of cheese for much less than five dollars including a drink. A note of warning; it is against the law to keep biting a sandwich while you are walking on the streets of Manhattan, although it is hardly enforced. While having lunch in one such cheap roadside outlets, one should be careful that one does not become the target of pick pockets.

Meat Production

As usual with America production of anything of public utilisation is usually conducted in a mass scale. Americans depend for their daily consumption on meat and poultry to a great extent. By statistics Americans consume most meat on a per capita basis in the world only next to Argentina. Besides by scientific analysis ecological concentration of energy is achieved through production of meat. Being endowed with vast acerages of land and huge length of coast lines America has the good fortune of producing meat and chicken in mass scale for the last few centuries. They abound in meat, fish and chicken production and the national habit of American's meat eating influences the national economy in a tremendous way. That makes the country surplus producer in agricultural produce. It spares non-meat agricultural produce for export to the world market. America's surplus economy in agriculture greatly depends on this concept. It results in surplus produce of rice, wheat, corn, soyabean and many other crops. One year's production of any one of the agricultural items can supply the whole worlds need for one year. If they accumulate the surplus production of several years America would run out of storage space. Stories of disposing of ship loads of grains like wheat and rice in the seas is true and happened in the United States. They try to prevent this on an annual basis. They have huge grain silos to hold the harvested agricultural produce for a few years, not indefinitely. Because they would run out of space in these holding silos. So Americans found some alternatives to this storage by discouraging over production of crops. The Government pays landed people not to produce crops on a portion of their lands. This concept of paying people not to produce food is unthinkable for others, particularly in India. But this is true in America. This also led to many corrupt practices where many rich farmers take undue advantage of the Government payment system by unfair means. A few countries like America, Australia and Canada which have means of huge agricultural production can unbalance the agricultural economy of the world by certain manipulations of the agricultural market. Big consumer societies like India, China and Russia have recently realized the significance of the role of consumers in the agricultural market. They have realized that they can not depend upon the surplus agricultural countries to dictate terms to them. This is only practicable if their own economies are self supporting or near so. China and Russia and most other countries of the world have lesser problems on this score because of their meat-eating habits. India's non meat- eating population stands in stark contrast to the rest of the world. It is surprising that even at the close of 20th century this is hardly recognised by the scientific Indians and less so by Indian politicians. India's problems can be analysed on scientific points of view if we have open minds. If we consider cattle as a source of key food in human society, India is very rich in food supply. However, majority of our people who are Hindus are biased against consumption of beef. The scientific communities and the politicians could open the minds of the religious people by research and recommendation of methods how to utilize these surplus cattle on a nationwide basis. Hindus do not have to eat against their wishes. However, they can allow people of other religions that inhabit India to eat cattle if they like. Hindus do not have to prohibit export of cattle to other countries for slaughter. The society and the Government can selectively make rules to reduce the number of unproductive cattle and subsidise the number of types of other animals which can be used for food purposes like goat, sheep and pigs. Cattle can be improved as to their milk production by import of foreign breeds and encouraging artificial breeding. Animal husbandry of other animals such as sheep, goats and pigs can be encouraged and subsidised particularly for the people of lower income groups. Intensive breeding of goats, sheep, pigs and chicken should be encouraged on a national basis.

Meat Inspection

Meat is the staple food of Americans. They enjoy most kinds of meat from animal sources. Primarily their meat food is from beef, pork, mutton and chicken. Recently some States have resources for marketing specialised meats from deer, bear and other wild or semi-wild animals. Thousands and thousands of animals are slaughtered everyday throughout America for meat purposes. So also millions and millions of chicken, ducks and smaller number of other birds. According to the laws of the United States all the meat including chicken and fish available for inter-state commerce in America must be inspected by U.S Government food inspectors. Majority of these inspectors are Veterinarians. There are other personnel which function as inspectors under the guidance of Veterinarians all over the United States. These Veterinary doctors get specialised training in meat inspection under the Federal Government. Most of the states have adopted Federal standards of meat inspection in their own jurisdiction. Since Americans depend on meat primarily for their daily diet, they pay much attention to the health and standards of the meat produced and their processing. They recognise many diseases which can be transmitted from animals to man through meat and meat products. Large number of animals have conditions which can transmit the disease to human beings. Even healthy animals can transmit certain disease to people if they are not handled in a clean and hygienic manner. Hence there is a reason for setting a standard of inspection of the meat production of these animals and birds which are meant for human consumption. In adition to their own consumption of meat in the United States, the country also exports large volume of meat and poultry to other countries which require healthy standards of meat production. This is why there is an extensive division of meat inspection in the agriculture department of the United States. This department employs thousands of Veterinarians and other professional and semiprofessional inspectors, which have to implement the inspection methods. I was a supervisory Veterinarian in this department before I retired. It is important to note that most Indian veterinary graduates can qualify for these jobs after clearing an examination and VISA qualification. The standards of meat inspection in America is geared for inspection of animals in large numbers. The animal carcasses, after they are slaughtered and bled, are hung up side down on big hooks which are moving at a particular speed by overhead trolleys. These carcasses are brought before the inspectors for variety of examinations. These inspectors are stationary, while the animal carcaces are moving. The speed of movement is set according to the manual of instruction allowing enough time for the inspectors to complete their inspection. Usually this takes a few minutes. If the inspector needs more time or suspects some disease in the animals he usually sidetracks the carcasses into an area which is called a "retained" area. The retained carcasses are evaluated further by veterinarians, who either pass or condemn them. If the veterinarians have further doubts they can retain or hold any of these carcaces for further tests in a refrigerated holding area. Chicken are slaughtered in large numbers in special slaughter houses for poultry. Basically the method of slaughter and inspection are similar to those of animals. The inspectors are standing at a particular station and chicken carcaces are moving in front of them at a particular speed, which is specified in the inspection manual. If the Inspector detects any abnormality in the individual chicken he can reject the whole chiken or part of it. If he has doubts he can keep for the final opinion the veterinarian. Although this is the summary of actions of the inspection system, the detailed procedures and guidelines are enumerated in thousands of pages of instructions in an inspection manual. To implement this inspection system and standard, the Federal govt. has the mandate from the Congress to implement these procedures with the help of scientific staff & methods. These inspectors are recognised and given due importance in protecting the health & economy of people of U.S.A. In spite of the fact that due to financial stringency, many compromises are recommended by the politicians and implemented by the scientific staff within the financial limits from time to time. Yet when health of the nation is at risk the govt. and the population at large give vocal and financial support to high standards of inspection. In spite of all these efforts many instances of failure of inspection standards do occur which cries out for remedial measures.

Milk Production

America is called the land of milk and honey. Over supply of milk in America is real. Individual cows producing hundred pounds of milk a day are not rare. These happen because of breeds with superior qualities of milk production from the strains of bulls and progeny of the cows of such high productivity. Unlike in India Americans have problem of over supply of milk in most areas. New York state is a state where there is an over supply of milk. The breed of cattle commonly in New York is Holstein, also known as Friesian. These animals originated in Europe but have been further improved on the American soil. Individual cows can be productive for about nine months of the year on an average. These animals look boney which is considered a desirable feature in the breed. A usual small farm in New York State has about fifty to hundred milch cattle. Most of them breed by artificial insemination. Majority of the bull calves are scarificed for meat purposes, after selecting a few good ones for breeding. These holstein cows can live upto fifteen years with average milking for about ten years. The other breeds of cattle selected for milk are Ayreshire and Jersey visible around North East. All over New York one would find small farms of Holstein cows, particularly in the spring, summer and fall these black and white cows in large numbers grazing in the countryside with a few large farm dogs inter mixed with them. Milk is pooled into big cooling Vats. The day's milk supply is stored in these chilling vats before further processing depending on the volume of days production. This milk is collected by big refrigerated tankers and transported to the central station where it is pasteurized and bottled for further distribution. Some of the surplus milk is further processed for butter and cheese production. Americans consume milk like water. Most young people and old people consume milk on a regular basis daily and are advised to do so. People who are more conscious of their weight consume low fat milk on regular basis. Americans have a problem with over weight and particularly after the age of thirty they have to be careful of their waistline. If you are a vegetarian you can enjoy your vegetarian life and have no problem in America if you have regular diet of milk and milk products. During the last thirty years there has been a marked decline in consumption of butter and whole milk. However, American society enjoys consuming milk rich diet daily which they think to be healthy. I believe that the statement of America being a land of milk and honey to be accurate as far as milk is concerned. Possibly honey would refer jointly to most of other food supplies. Most children have three glasses of milk a day, one for breakfast, one at lunch and one before bed time. Most old people would have a glass of milk at least at bed time. Other adults have regular milk habits too.

America has always been a great place in the minds of Indians particularly after we got independence. Large number of Indians have gone to America and also large numbers have settled down. There is a great excitement in the minds of Indians to go to America for visit or study or for permanent residence.

Immigration To America

Compared to most countries of the world America holds a great deal of appeal as a heaven for economic prosperity. This is not imaginary but real. Because of two factors: the huge size of the country and low population. Although these vast lands three hundred years ago were unexplored, in the recent century. Its natural resources have been tapped for the benefit of American society and also for the benefit of the human society as a whole. Vast resources of American economy has come to the rescue of the world's population at various times both in War and in Peace and still doing so. During the last half of twentieth century America has made great strides in various spheres of human endeavor. Most attractive to the outside world are the features of America's system which sign as beacon for economic prosperity of human beings depending on individual enterprise. People all over the world have always been attracted by this beacon to come to the shores of America in search of better life. It is a fact not fantasy that America provides great opportunity for millions and millions of people from all over the world for better life in its borders. There is a huge statue in the harbour of New York with inscription inviting people from all over the world beginning with these statements. "Give me your poor and hungry..... This invitation to the whole world to send its hungry millions to America has remained a constant offer, although modified by present times. There is a stream of immigration to America continuously with several million people coming here every year, more than half of them to live in this country bearianently. These people who are allowed beally five in America are the few blessed ones by God because these people multiply their earning ability by hundred times or more. They can live in a society of plenty of everything, food and other necessities, without any quota systern at all on any goods, American people consume all the human needs like water. They consume electricity possibly at the rate of hundred times per capita consumption of Indians. They consume gasoline and oil and its byproducts a thousand fold compared to Indians. The food volume and variety available at a very cheap price are incomparable in the world. If we are consuming meat and fish once or twice a week, they consume meat or fish or chicken as their daily staple diet. Meat is served as the main dish in the middle of the plate with other side dishes. Milk and milk products are enjoyed similarly. Because of these varying socioeconomic considerations the world provides a stream of applicants who would like to come to America without end. America's laws and rules have been modified from time to time for accommodating this rush of hungry millions from the outside world. In 1965 President Johnson made revolutionary changes in the immigration laws allowing large number of immigrants from most countries of the world. Prior to that India used to have a quota of only a hundred immigrants a year but under Johnson's rule it became twenty thousand. In adition to this twenty thousand, dependents of citizens and other priority class immigrants are allowed outside the quota. Johnson's quota provided a numerical limit of seven hundred fifty thousand immigrants from all over the world not including the non quota Individuals. Recent laws have somewhat tightened these total numbers to around six hundred thousand basic immigrants. Inspite of very recent restrictive trend during the last two congresses, the basic liberal system allowing half million to one million legal immigrants a year has remained. The system will also consider for immigration of certain qualified people if it can be proven that they are being discriminated in their parent county, such as persecuted minorities in a society. Many Sikhs have successfully sought refugee status under this formula. The following categories of people can apply for favourable consideration under the American immigration Laws.

FIRST CATEGORY

(1) Highly educated people who have attained eminence in their own nation and society. This can

include prominent people in sciences, Art, literature performing Arts or any learned profession.
(2) Highly educated people who have established their eminence in the world or American society.
(3) People who are religious clerics.
(4) (a) Dependants of American citizens. Such people include married or unmarried, their spouses and their minor children.
(b) Parents of American citizen if living abroad.
(5) Immediate dependents of immigrant green card holders who are not yet American citizens. This includes the unmarried children and parents of such green card holders.
(6) Refugees who have been persecuted by a society. Usually this number is outside the quota limits.
(7) Any other person who can prove as a descendant of any group or individual who had a prior claim of residential rights in America.
(8) Any person who has certain claims of having served in the United States defence forces.

These are some of the brief classifications of people qualifying for immigrant status in America. A person seeking immigrant VISA in America can seek the advice of specific lawyers specializing in immigrant matter. There are many law firms in most big cities of America dealing with these matters. There are also several law firms in India to deal with immigration to Canada and America. Anybody wishing to go to America should first visit the American embassy in New Delhi or its consulates located in Calcutta, Bombay and Madras. They can also write to these agencies, offices for advice and instruction. Even if they do not fulfil any of the priority categories mentioned above, they can still apply on approved forms to be filed with the American embassy for listing their names for any future vacancies in the quota. A note of caution in quota for Indians: the quota for Indian immigrant VISA is closed as over subscribed for many years at this time.

Second Category

These VISAs are granted to people who want to visit America for temporary periods.

Tourists, Business Promoters and Family Visitors

This is the biggest group of people visiting America. They are like people who visit different places in their vacation time or visit friends and relatives and explore possibilities of business connections with the individuals or companies. Such people usually own funds sufficient enough for them to spend time in America. They must establish that they have roots in India which will bring them back to this country. Many people who go to America as temporary visitors end up staying in America for much longer periods of time. Some of these people try to take legal help to get their stays extended to indefinite period. Many just stay on beyond their authorized periods. This is illegal until they get the immigration permit. The immigration system employs large number of inspectors to catch hold of these violators. When they catch these violators the penalty can be severe like immediate imprisonment depending on the circumstances of the case. Any one who is caught in this situation having violated his basic period of stay without any reasonable cause is advised to immediately seek competent legal help from one of the firms dealing with immigration matters. An ordinary lawyer is not recommended. If there is a reasonable cause which can be established by the lawyer then the immigration office will grant certain period of extension of time for one to three months before the parties are allowed to depart America without penalty. If legal representation is not enough or the immigration authorities are not convinced of the genuineness of the circumstances, they usually, put these people in immigration prison, while their cases are being examined by the courts. Therefore, it is advised for those who intentionally lengthen their stay in America beyond the authorized period should either be in correspondence with the immigration office or be represented by competent legal help. If you are in correspondence with the immigration office asking for extension of stay and your authorized stay has expired then there is no penalty. Usually the letter from the immigration will either permit you to overstay as you have applied for or give you a time by which you should depart the United States. If you want to appeal against their decision and further request extension of stay, it is better that this is done by a lawyer in the United States on your behalf. Once the matter is handled by a lawyer the immigration people do not take any drastic action, because most of these immigration people are lawyers who deal with immigration matters have also worked in the immigration department for some time in the past. If by any chance any of these visitors insist on staying in America permanently one way is to marry an American citizen or American permanent resident, which will permit the applicant a permanent resident status. However, it must be genuine marriage. If it is not genuine marriage and somehow this is detected by the immigration department, one is liable to be immediately deported and the other permanent resident of America is liable for prosecution under immigration laws. Therefore, recently many dependent spousal immigrant VISAS are granted for a maximum period of two years after which time it is reviewed if the two spouses are still living together or not. Many people try to deceive the immigration system while applying for various types of authorization. It is highly desirable for people who consider that their future interests are in the United States do not deal with immigration system in a deceptive way. Such acts of deception are very commonly resorted to by people of south American countries, Middle East etc. Indians still are involved in a smaller number of such deceptive cases, many have been caught and penalized. Therefore, it is highly desirable that respectable people behave in a law abiding way in America. Because the legal manpower in America is extensive compared to what people know in India and can overpower such law breakers before they know it.

Student Visas

This is one category of VISA in which large number of people from all other countries are admitted to U.S.A. There are a few requirements for this.

(a) You must get admission to a university for under graduate or post graduate course of study.

(b) You must have sufficient funds at your disposal in bank account or somebody in America will give you guarantee of monetary support to the extent of your stay at least for one year. If these two basic conditions are met the consulate or the embassy will usually give you non immigrant VISA for the period of study at your college. But the number of applications for this VISA from India are so huge, in this category that the embassy and the consulates do not approve your student status automatically. They try to read your application between the lines and if there is suspicion that you could possibly overstay in America and look for opportunities for permanent residence, then they do not approve the student VISA. The authority of these consular officers in granting or rejecting these VISAs is usually final unless the American Ambassador in the country specially intervenes, which he rarely does. Once your application is rejected by one consulate under this suspicion, the information is computerised and available for other consulates in the country. In the past student VISAs were granted almost automatically. Now-a-days about half the cases are refused on the basis of suspicion of the consular offices about the genuineness of your purpose in education. The consulates have been given discretionary powers in regard to grant of these temporary VISA in any category. This can not be appealed except to the Ambassador. It can not be appealed to any agency of the U.S.A. Govt. beyond the Ambassador's level. It is therefore recommended that for a person to succeed in getting a student VISA to America takes all actions legitimately to provide proof of proper study and also genuineness of funds available. If you can prove that, you are eligible for this kind of study at more than one institution in America with supporting papers then your case may be stronger. If you are a good student as per the Indian University records with multiple recommendation letters from different educational institutions which you have attended, your case will be more impressive to the Consulate officers. If your scholastic background is first class or above, this can also be impressive. It is important that these performances should be consistent to prove your scholarly background. It is better to have some practical experience in the Indian situation in the area of your choice. Most of the American colleges and universities provide opportunity for practical work in the areas where possible. If you have some practical experience in the field in India, it usually adds to the confidence of the candidates in the particular discipline. Sometimes these practical experiences prove and improve upon ones academic knowledge and experience. Therefore, in summary a student seeking foreign training in America immediately after his academic degrees is considered less prepared than somebody who has had a few years of practical experience. A Doctor or Veterinarian should have one year of internship and few years of training in a particular specialty involving practical experience. Such multiple years of training and experience can be completed in a residency programme. Or a Post Graduate degree with two or three years of Post Graduate training may be satisfactory substitute in that field. Other scientists and engineers should have a similar period of proven experience. In non science areas a few years of experience in any kind of teaching or research position may be suitable substitute. The position of teaching should be in the subject of specialisation or be allied to it. It will also be in the interest of the candidate to make available any proof of one's good facility and proficiency in English language, particularly with a letter of commendation from an English Professor who has personal knowledge of the candidate. If the English Professor has been trained in America, Canada or England it will be more impressive.

In summary one must present at the first encounter with the evaluating officers of the embassy or the Universities that the record of performances of the applicant is superior and sincere. This would appeal to the appraiser for a kinder and more favourable review. However, all statements made in the applications should be true and can be proven if questioned. Americans have usually a pink eye while appraising letters of recommendation of candidates from underdeveloped countries and countries like India. Many people have a misconception that most of the recommendation letters are not based on facts and are deceptive. If one or more recommendation letters are available from individuals who have had training in America that would be helpful. Sending out applications for possible admissions to a few universities or colleges is advised. At least four applications should be made to different geographical areas. If a candidate has ability to transmit his applications to more institutions, it is OK, but it can be expensive. Application to less famous universities and colleges can bear fruit easier. The process of application, their review and receipt of the results of the decisions of the Universities can be time consuming and can take upto three to four months or longer. So one must have patience and time to wait for the decisions.

Immigration And Naturalisation Service (Ins) Of Us Govt.

INS is the part of the department of Justice of the American government. They have jurisdiction over all foreigners entering and leaving the United States. The department controls by various means and various subject agencies entrance and legalization of foreigners in America. They also have surveillance on the movement of foreigners in America. They have full jurisdiction of authorisation of stay in America of any foreigner. If a foreigner violates his authorization they have a system to apprehend and put him in jail while his status is being examined. Any foreigner visiting America must have a valid VISA which authorises him or her for stay for a particular period of time. If he has exceeded that authorized period he is in violation of federal rules of immigration. If the expiry has happened only by a few days you should immediately report with an application for further stay to the immigration department. If it has been accidental usually there is no problem. If it is intentional and for long period then the immigration department may penalise you. Such penalty may land you in jail. If by accident you have over-stayed for a long period it is better to take the advice of a lawyer dealing with immigration laws. Temporary VISAs are granted under various circumstances such as travelling or visiting friends and relatives in America or exploring business opportunities in America, for study in schools and colleges in America etc. These temporary VISAs can be granted for varying periods from three months to the extent of study periods in the universities. After completion of study, one year of VISA is available for gaining practical experience. There are many detailed rules and regulations which one has to comply with for each kind of VISA. Indians are advised to remain within legal limits of their stay in USA as per their VISA, Those who are bold enough to face the untoward circumstances as a result of violation of the VISA rules may do so at their own risk. Because the first penalty by the immigration service is imprisonment in their jail which is located in the same office. Once imprisoned by the immigration service the courts and the laws of the locality have no powers to intervene. Only the Federal Government and Federal legal system have any jurisdiction over them. The office and the personnel of the immigration department are not usually available over the weekends. So if a person is in the custody of the immigration office on friday, there is no way to release him until monday. The office and the staff of the immigration and naturalisation service are very insensitive to the appeals of the people they deal with. Because they think they are dealing with unwanted foreigners. This can present a difficult situation for a foreigner who may be highly respectable in his own land but that does not make any difference to the INS. They deal with them very impersonally. So it is advised that foreigners while dealing with the immigration and naturalisation service should be always careful that they do not violate immigration rules on a serious basis and they should be careful to have recourse to a lawyer dealing with immigration laws. Once you are protected by consulting an immigration lawyer then the immigration people become more careful. They will not venture to illtreat you or put you in immigration prison so easily, because they are cautious of the lawyers. The lawyers in America have more powers than their counterparts in India. With certain limitations as to their jurisdiction, lawyers can act as judges in many instances. They also have other special powers from the judges. Under these circumstances the lawyers are not treated as ordinary pleaders for their clients but they have their own rights and privileges. Therefore, once a lawyer is involved in a case the immigration system handles them with softness and deliberation. An experience of a foreigner in the immigration ofice in New York city can be harrowing. For everything related with immigration office there is a printed form with numbers at the bottom. You have to get that form to apply for any particular purpose. Every form has to be asked for by a number printed at the bottom of the form. If you are lucky to know the number of the forms you can get them by mail, but you must have enough time at your disposal. Easily it may take one to two weeks for the form to arrive. Many foreigners dont have too much time at their disposal to ask for these forms. They think it is easier to visit the INS office personally & pick up the forms. When one visits the INS office to pick up the forms in New York city it may be early hours of the office between 9 & 10, but you find that the lines for any business in the INS office has already become almost a quarter mile long, then you have to join the line. Several hundred people ahead of you have to be disposed off before your turn comes. This initial visit to pick up the forms may take half day to full day. You return home with the forms to appropriately fill it. If you are lucky & mail the form immediately then within a week you will get in the mail the necessary forms for your purpose. You have to take time to fill up that form accurately and submit by mail. If you are applying for extension of your stay you may have to enclose evidence of money order of a cheque of a specified amount that is payable. This must be the exact amount. You have to write down the form number at the top of the cheque or the money order and your name specifying the purpose for which the fee is being paid. The fee once paid is never returned, even if the action applied for is not complied with. In spite of the fact that contacts with the immigration office for any item can appear very harassing. most of the time, things get done. You may not get the response readily or without waiting in the line for hours, but you will get the response in time. The waiting in line or the waiting for the response to arrive are due to the fact that there is a great demand for their services but there are only a smaller number of employees. These appear to be the case during recent years. This may be due to the fact that large number of applicants for service at the INS office and fewer number of employees at the same office because of financial restrictions. In summary all foreigners have to deal with this INS office frequently. It is better that they remain informed of the rules & regulations of this department. It is better to work do through the mails. But these have to be done ahead of time, keeping about at least two weeks in your hand. If you have less time, it is better to go through the torture of personally visiting the immigration office. Once a completed form is in the hands of the immigration office before expiry of the VISA status or other matter, you are safe. In important cases where you are not sure of getting things done by yourself, it is better to engage an immigration lawyer also giving him intimation much ahead of time. For instance, if you are applying for the change of status of one VISA to another and the current VISA expires in about a month. This is the time to contact the lawyer to represent your case at the immigration office. Once the lawyer starts corresponding with the immigration office, you are safe. Even if the INS office refuses to allow your prayer, they will give you and your lawyer enough time about three months for any remedial action.

It is advised that all foreigners should develop a conforming attitude and not a confrontational attitude while dealing with the INS department. If you take time to willingly comply with their requirements you have done your job and hope for more positive answer. If you develop a confrontational attitude in complying with the requirements of the INS instructions, then you have only created antagonistic response. One has to clearly understand that while applying for certain privileges with the INS, you are only asking for their kind accommodation and not as a matter of right, because you are a foreigner.

Educational Opportunities In America

Of all the English speaking countries, America provides the largest number of colleges and universities in any one country. There are literally thousands of colleges in America and hundreds of universities. These colleges and universities have variety of academic programmes that offer under graduate and graduate degrees. These academic programmes include almost all subjects in the Arts, Sciences and other applied disciplines of human knowledge. Majority of the colleges and universities have advanced programmes in basic sciences of biology. Chemistry, physics. Mathematics, Arts and literature and large number of them have programmes in Medicine, agriculture including Veterinary science, computer science and management sciences like business management and hotel management. These academic programmes are described in further detail in hand books published by the universities and colleges. Since they are bulky you do not expect thern to be easily mailed to you by international postal system. If it is essential for you to have access to these books called academic catalogues of specific colleges it is advisable if you ask some personal friends to acquire them from the universities and mail them to you. Most of the foreign students do not have access to these bulky catalogues while applying for admission. If one applies to a university giving indication of one of the area of his specialisation and degree he is seeking, the university will mail forms to him and abstracts of bulky books of the relevant sections for his guidance. They also send advisory letters on the subject to follow up and the persons to contact. Attached to the American embassy and the consulate there are educational attaches who also have libraries with catalogues of various American Universities. You can apply giving your specific desire and goal of study. They can give you further possible guidance. American University and Colleges are not only in the business of educating people in America but also they have a goal of making an income from the foreign sources for furtherance of their educational programmes in America. American Education at the university level has become extremely expensive during the last twenty years. Therefore, their college fees and related expenses have gone very high. For example a programme in sciences that would have cost three thousand dollars a year in 1960 has gone upto about twenty five thousand at current times. This inflation has affected both American and foreign students. Some colleges which are state supported have lesser charges for the people of the state than for outsiders. The fee charged to foreigners are usually the highest. On an average most American colleges and the universities would cost about twenty thousand American dollars a year. One would be lucky to find the college where the total expenses for the year would be ten to twelve thousand dollars. This inflation in the expenses of American education has discouraged large number of students, particularly those of modest means from the main stream college education. There are many vocational Institutes and colleges which offer two to four years programmes in variety of discipline. These are greatly in the demand. Because most of them are less expensive and are supported by the state governments. These are usually taught at two year colleges which are situated almost all over the country. Most of them are conducted by the states and the fees charged are lowest amongst the college system. If one wants specialised vocational training in these two year colleges he or she can get them cheaply through some of these institution. Although their progrmmes offer only a Diploma at the end of two years, there is no loss in the quality of the education offered. If foreigners would want to take advantage of this two year programme it will be an excellent way of getting an American education inexpensively. Most of these two year colleges have authorization for enrolling foreign students like regular colleges.

Four Year Colleges

These colleges provide the backbone of the American college education system. They may be affiliated to universities or function independently. There are some famous colleges in America which have remained independent of any university affiliation for centuries. Some of these provide highly academic programmes in Arts and Sciences offering only one degree of Bachelor of Arts. After completion of the degree of Bachelor of Arts from such colleges most students go on to universities to pursue courses of study in medicine, Arts or other sciences.

Universities

American Universities in most parts are residential universities in contrast to the concept of affiliating universities in India. These universities offer educational programmes in a campus set up. The Campus have various colleges and departments offering specific programmes. Most of these colleges in university campus have their own curriculum for one or more degrees granted by the college. Bulk of the courses in these degree colleges are offered intramurally. These colleges offer their basic degrees depending on courses such as agriculture, veterinary medicine, human medicine, engineering etc. For graduate students there is freedom for choosing certain courses from any other college or department depending on the need of the students and the advice of the graduate advisory committee. For conducting the Post Graduate degree programmes involving one college or more colleges in the campus, the responsibility and authority are usually vested in schools called graduate school of the university. The graduate school has the jurisdiction to offer any degree higher than the bachelor degree or the basic degree of the professional schools, such as M.D. or D.V.M. In America usually there is no limit to the número of colleges and universities, as long as funds are available for the programme. Usually there is one major state university campus in each state. In addition to this there are large number of colleges and universities which have been privately funded. There is still control and supervisory responsibility over these universities at the level of the state government. The state education department has the role to supervise the programmes of these colleges and Universities if their programmes are according to certain guidelines stated as per the state constitution. These Universities and their constituent colleges are also supervised by the respective professional societies controlling that particular professional college, such as medical society, guiding the medical colleges, Law society, guiding the programmes of the Law colleges.

Funding Of Educational Institutions

Most of the state colleges and universities which have the basic role of providing education to the masses are funded by the state government and some local governments. However, large number of colleges and universities in America have been initiated and maintained by private funds. These private funds have usually started with wealthy individuals, later on supported by other sources. Many of these universities and colleges bear the names of the founders. These non-governmental institutions are in large number, in most of the American cities and some in other rural areas. The funds that support these colleges and universities are tax exempt which encourages individual fund givers. Another big agency that provides funds for non-governmental educational programmes are the religious organisations. Particularly the Catholic Church is very active and very prominent in this regard. Huge universities are funded by tax exempt religious organisations. These Churches also make sure to acknowledge with thanks the donations of individual givers. Many medical hospitals and entire medical colleges are founded by such charitable organisations. All non-government organisations still have to conform to the requirements of the state education department as regards the quality of education and other basic requirements. About half the post high school, non- governmental education institutions in America are funded by these sources. At the high school level funding of these educational institutions administered by the religious organisation also get part of their expenses through the government. In general huge sums of money are spent in education in these post high school institutions either through the government or through private agencies. To name a few, Columbia University, Cornell University, New York University, Catholic University in New York, Yeshiva University in New York, Fordham University in New York, each of which is a huge organisation enrolling several thousand students are examples of private Universities in New York city. Needless to say the standards of these private Universities are at the tops. Examples of other private

Universities of high repute outside New York are Princeton in New Jersey, Harvard in Massachusetts and Standford in California. In the last half of the twentieth Century American higher education has become more expensive but more standardized. Some of these small colleges under the impact of tightness of funding have merged with bigger Universities. During the last twenty years there has been tightness of Federal monetary support for many of the programmes of the colleges, that has resulted in increase of tuition and other charges imposed on the students. However, a review of the total picture of the college world would reveal that a few weaker colleges have reduced their programmes or merged with bigger universities but in general American Universities and Colleges are still going strong at more places. Weaker programmes and students with less scholastic abilities have separated out into junior colleges that are called Community Colleges which offer mostly a two year programme. Most of these junior colleges are meant for mass education and are funded by the government. These two year colleges have taken over the responsibility of educating the masses that support the societies programmes on a current basis, leaving the role of teaching to the graduates and post graduates of the universities. There is a great deal of emphasis of educating the new crops of younger people in this two year system which is relatively less expensive. The programme is financially supported by the Federal Government and operated by the state and local governments.

Business And Other Opportunities In America

Large number of people wishing to go abroad have gone to enter into business opportunities in America, primarily in a collaborative manner. People who are permanent residents in America either green card holders or citizens can be interested in setting up business themselves in America. Other visitors can explore possibilities of collaborating with American counterparts in any kind of business effort. One common effort is to try to sell Indian textiles in America. Exploring opportunities for exporting handicrafts, work of Arts and other engineering products through established business houses, particularly Indian owned business houses are recommended. In spite of big publicity by America and other developed countries in the world of opening trade facilities to all the under developed countries in the world, there seems to be no sincere desire to help the under developed countries of the world. The underlying desire seems to be to sell more goods and services from the stronger economies to the weaker ones. Despite lack of need for such commerce in these under developed societies, these efforts under the guise of liberatlisation appear to be predominantly to sell goods and services from the more economically developed countries to the lesser ones. The stronger economic powers of the world are not suddenly sympathetic and kind to the needs of the under developed societies. Their primary goal is based on selfish motivation to sell goods and services from their countries at a profit. Since these advanced countries have machinery and organisations that promote their products and services all over the world, such efforts ultimately and strongly beneficial to the developed Societies. Although they are marginally beneficial to the developing ones, it the ünder developed economies do not keep various safeguards to protect their own interests if is only a matter of time that the developing world will be over powered and over dependent on the developed societies. Many recent actions of the United States and other powerful industrial nations of the world have provided immense proof for their intentions to dominate the world economy in these matters. It is therefore, essential that less advanced societies and countries of the world have to be careful in analyzing the effects of such over penetrasion by the economic super powers which would be almost tantamount to subjugation of such society by force. India, China and other populous yet not advanced societies are in this category. By recent analysis of the programmes of opening of the economy, China presents a very watchful and guarded situation in the world, where as India has been embracing the open system with open arms, India's democratic system of divided allegiance of the electorate to various nation building programmes stands in contrast to the monolithic dictatorial system in China. India is subject to more subversion whereas China is not. In connection with this open world business Indian economy has to be careful and introspective about the benefits of over liberalization of these programmes. In a final analysis India's balance of trade is behind in serious negative side can be highly detrimental to the already poor economy of country. So these considerations should be a vital ones at the national level, and at the level of the planning commission while formulating their plans. In accepting or rejecting any particular economic plan or proposal advanced by the advanced economic powers of the world very detailed considerations of the repercussions of these proposals should be analysed before any action is taken On the surface certain proposals sals may appear good from humane consideration on a worldwide basis but accepting those proposals by poor countries like India has to be adjudged on the basis of the realities of life existing. For example prohibition of child labour. Ideally child labour laws should prevent child labour and should encourage children to attend schools for education but if at home child's poor parents can not provide two square meals to the family and the child contributes to the family by working during the day, the world should not impose the restriction on the family to send the child to school who is hungry. Developed countries have built in programmes of personal allowances for families who have no source of income, so that they can have their basic food and shelter available to them. However, this is not available in the present Indian system to the poor people. Still millions of people go hungry on a daily basis, many of them resorting to all kinds of methods of survival including begging, prostitution and child labour. So what is wrong with a hungry child to do some work to support himself or part of his family's needs as long as the society is blind and unable to provide them the basic support? The more affluent countries of the world have imposed this concept of banning child labour on poorer societies without solving the hunger problem of the world. You have no business to tell a child or his parents not to do any gainful work and die of hunger. Where is the logic of bringing a hungry child from earning his meals by any legitimate work ? We can only enforce our standards over such people of the society after solving their basic needs.

Therefore, India's economic realities need to focus on some of these basic needs prior to accepting these idealistic concepts of preventing child Jabour. They should first ensure a family an allowance for providing the minimum requirement of food and shelter for poor people. Second, there should be a system of social security for the old and retired. It is desirable that they do not starve and become homeless. Before ensuring these plans for prohibition of child labour, other undesirable features should be taken care of.

Many Indians and Indian businesses can benefit from their association with existing houses of business in America either under the ownership of Indians or otherwise. These Indian business should not only concentrate their activities on selling and marketing Indian handicrafts, but they should try to market industrial goods and machinery manufactured in India in the foreign market. Theoretically cost of production of these goods and services in India being lower, they can be sold competitively in the more advanced economic societies easily and with bigger profit margins. You have to sell what they need; that should be the general concept. If they need Ph.Ds in Mathematics and Physics, you should supply them as you are doing under H-1 VISA. If they need domestic workers, you should explore avenues of providing them. You should also explore opportunities for selling things in America competitively, the goods and services which America also produces like Japan did. The Japanese made a marketing research to find out what are the topmost needs in American society. They observed that the car was the essential need in America. They produced some excellent, cars for American market, which were even priced higher than their American counter-parts. Even then more Japanese cars were sold than the American manufactured ones. So that should be the goal of Indian industry while selling to the world. We should manufacture finished goods which the western society needs and try to sell them at a competitive price. Then we can claim that India has succeeded.

On a practical basis India can capitalise on certain positive features of Indian economy. India has large number of surplus manpower who are educated in science, liberal Arts and technologies and in English. These are great assets. They should be marketed with active support from the Government and other non-Governmental organisations.

Selling the educational system to the needy societies in the world can not only result in economic productivity of Indian education, but also spreading the educational philosophy of India in such countries. Luckily there are huge geographic regions in the world which can utilise the Indian manpower, such as America, Canada, England, Australia, New Zealand, and many countries in Africa which speak English. We do not have to only think of selling goods to the outside world, we should sell the surplus manpower who are trained in India in English to the societies mentioned above. India should become one of the centres of education in the world, particularly for English speaking people. Marketing of goods of Indian produce and manufacture: this is a more visible concept in the export trade. We should try to encourage as much export as possible without providing any significant protection to such trades so that the manufacturers can compete in the world market. At the same time we should facilitate programmes of export. Taxing system and duties system should be made favourable for such programmes.

Opportunity For Medical Scientists In America: Medicare And Other Health Programmes

America spends the largest budget item in the Federal Govt. on raedical care of its people. The Federal government spends annually hundreds of billions dollars on "Medicare". This Medicare programme provides healthcare facilities for the elderly and their dependents. People who qualify for this programme are the ones who have paid premiums throughout their life time. Matching premiums have been paid by the federal government. There is a schedule of fees payable under these plans to the medical doctors and the hospitals that take care of these beneficiaries. At current times about forty per cent of American population depend on this programme. Majority of these people are old and retired. But this plan also includes large number of dependents and other beneficiaries who are young. This programme started in 1960s as a very small but benevolent programme by the federal government that saw the old and retired people were neglected because they had no insurance for medical care. Within about twenty five years this programme has grown into the biggest item of expenditure in the federal budget. The government is struggling continuously to control expenditure on "Medicare" but have not succeeded yet. Beside "Medicare" there is a huge programme for providing medical care for the poor who are not able to provide for themselves. This programne would roughly provide for fifteen to twenty per cent of the people. The cost of this programme is borne by the federal and the state governments which again is a major area of expenditure of the government budget. In addition to these two programmes there is the regular health insurance programme availed by the largest segment of population in America that are currently employed. This programme is funded by contribution of the employers and employees on equal basis. All these three health insurance programmes mentioned above are huge operations employing millions of people and thousands of medical doctors and other scientists. This extensive system of medical industrial complex as is called by some segments provide immense opportunity for medical and allied scientists openings for jobs and practice positions. Indian doctors, nurses, pharmacists and other allied health professionals are very suitable and eligible for consideration for employment in this medical industrial complex. However, there are many road blocks for entry of foreigners into this system. But once the foreigners enter into this system they can succeed according to their ability without any limits. Road blocks have been intentionally created by the legislators who feel many foreigners are unfairly taking the opportunities away from the Americans. Otherside of the story is that the system has positions for thousands and thousands of people who if admitted can help the system and ultimately the American economy. So from time to time, in spite of certain restraints of the tightening laws of the federal government large number of doctors and scientists in allied disciplines are allowed to enter U.S.A. and ultimately remain in the country permanently. These people when qualified attain highest levels of incomes in the country. These incomes are almost guaranteed by the system of "Medicare", welfare and other health insurance programmes. How can one qualify for going to America under these medical programmes ?

By and large a doctor or a nurse or a paramedic has to qualify by certain examinations. This examination is offered from time to time in various countries of the world (at this time India does not have any examination centres for medical scientists). So any Indian desirous of taking this opportunity has to go outside India for taking these examinations. These examinations are held in Pakistan, Srilanka and Singapore regularly to mention a few of the neighboring countries. An Indian medical scientist or a nurse can take advice for this examination from the U.S. embassy or consulate, in India and in the countries where the examinations are held. This examination is a must and has to be completed successfully by any medical scientist before applying for admission to the U.S.A..

There are other examinations which also have to be fulfilled. One important examination is called TOEFL. This is a test for proficiency in English. Most Indian scientists and doctors would easily qualify under this test but they have to sit for one of the examinations at one of these centres in India. India still allows TOEFL centres to conduct examinations in various cities of the country. If one succeeds in this medical qualifying examination then one is eligible for entry into the medical programmes in America. But there are many more obstructions which still stand on the way. Indian government does not allow medical doctors to avail of these opportunities in America. They have restrictions on doctors to leave the country. Besides the American government also has temporary restriction on these doctors to get VISA to come to America from certain countries like India. This is because of the pressures of the Indian government on America not to give VISAS to these medical scientists. In spite of all these restrictions many Indians with medical qualifications do succeed in gaining entry in the United States in many tortuous ways.

Ways To Get Entry Into The U.S.A.:

One way is to try to get a VISA as a visitor to America without mentioning your qualifications, affiliations etc. After reaching there you contact the appropriate agencies to assess your qualifications for employment VISA.

If a person who is medically qualified is able to qualify

as a citizen or permanent resident of America, he can also get VISA to go to America without any restriction. For example, if the medical doctor is a citizen by birth because his parents were in America at the time of his birth then he gets automatic citizenship. If a person has been admitted as a green card holder and is having a permanent VISA which has not expired then he can go to USA without any restriction.

H-1 VISA: For this VISA one has to be employee of an Indian Company doing business in America or an American company giving employment to this individual for temporary periods. These people, are usually granted H-1 VISAS. Their stay is usually limited to six years. They can however adjust their status to other kinds of VISAS or permanent VISA under certain circumstances.

Exchange Visitor VISA: This VISA is allowed for scientists and medical personnel who are of proven eminence by virtue of their education, training, experience etc. This VISA is limited to six years but does not allow adjustment of status under other kinds of VISA during or after expiry of their stay. If such a person gets an offer to remain permanently in the USA he is not allowed to do so. He has to leave the country for at least two years before he is allowed to come back. However, there may be certain exceptions which can qualify him to stay on. Such exceptions include marriage to an American citizen or a permanent resident.

In spite of all the restrictions of government of India and of the USA on the medical scientists many people still get entry into the USA if they have persistence in their efforts and if they satisfy minimum qualifications.

Advantages Of An Indian In America

The first advantage an Indian in America has is his fluency in English. If he speaks good English, understands and writes correct English it is a very strong advantage. Because the bulk of Americans speak english. Most Indians speak English with accent which distorts the language by American standard. So it is advised that one should speak the language slowly and try to speak it clearly, so that the influence of the accent will be less. During the first few months of stay in America Indians should consciously try to develop and practise American accent English. Then they will be more intelligible. A short course in spoken english from any of the colleges, particularly from junior colleges can be very useful. Often the Indians do not realise this deficiency that they are not being understood well. They go in their own way of speaking and speaking as fast as possible and assume that the world is going to understand them. But this can be improved by taking a short course in spoken English. Most Indians who are not very good at English, particularly those who have not gone beyond basic college level should take courses in English for one or two semesters. One need not feel small to make efforts to improve one's power of delivery of speech. Most Indians can improve their advantage in English language by taking these short courses in spoken American English.

Those people who do not take this remedial course may suffer in the long run. However, majority of Indians I have met in various campuses do very well in the language area.

Indian Consulates

There are four Indian consular offices in America. One with the Indian embassy in Washington D.C. and one in each city of New York, Chicago and San Francisco. There are specific regions of America which are served by these consular offices. The primary role of these consular offices is to renew the passport of Indians in America and granting of VISAS to non- Indians for their travel to India. Indian passports are now available for ten-year periods. Indians in America can renew their passports if expired by going to the local Indian consulates. If you are a visitor and your passport has expired, you have to give an additional proof of your financial ability and purpose of your stay etc. The consular office also grants VISAS on foreign passports. Currently American passport holders can have a VISA for continuous stay of five years which can be extended later in India if necessary. The functions of the Indian consulates are to help Indians in America who need help in establishment and facilitation of businesses in the country. There is also an educational attachee to advise the students visiting or trying to get admission in Indian universities.

How Indians Succeed in America

There are a few ways a man can succeed in life. Hard work keeping a few goals definite in mind; developing a discipline in one's daily life. Making most of one's talents. In adition to these abstract features one's success and failure also are dependent on the environment. A favourable environment can be very beneficial and helpful, whereas an unfavorable environment can diminish the productivity of individual or destroy it. Majority of the people who succeed in going to America are spectacularly endowed with such special talents. They may have other assets like financial and manpower etc. America provides greatest opportunity to those who do hard work. Hard work does not only include out door physical labour. One can work very hard mentally. American environment provides a very fertile field for the right individual to be productive and prosperous. Such individuals can prosper in the field of academics, business, medicine, or in the other learned professions like law, management and sciences. The person has to choose the best area for his specialisation. You will have to survey the American business and economic situations before you jump into any particular activity or you may have natural talent for certain area which you love and specialise America provides immense opportunity for Indians to succeed if they are talented and hard working. Most of the time people who want to make quick money by cheating and other nefarious activities usually do not succeed in the long run. Besides, America provides enough opportunity for making a solid living by honest means and honest efforts. So those Indians who have gone to America and have sincere desire to succeed by fair means and hard work, they will, because America provides ample opportunity for that. Most of the successful Indians in America are amongst the educated people. Majority of them in medicine and others are in learned professions. Since the history of Indians in America is very recent, success of other people in the business world has not yet come to the fore, although large number of Indians in America are in business. We will be knowing more of them in the future decades. But at the present time it appears that most of the successful people of Indians who have come to the forefront have done so by their hard work. If you are hard worker and moderately intelligent, America beckons you to come. America provides great opportunities for success for every individual, native or immigrant. The resources, natural and man-made are immense. The pioneers had planned to exploit the natural resources in a very intelligent and deliberate manner, so that the future generations would keep enjoying their lives almost indefinitely. The various agencies of the federal and state governments are also conservative in their minds. They utilise the resources and plan to preserve those resources on a continuing basis. The basic laws of the land are very favourable for conservation of these resources. Because of the vast size of the country and long coastlines of non freezing water, the natural resources seem to be endless. The continuous efforts of the American society to extract maximum utilization of any particular resource has endowed America continuing vastness of its original resources. If there is dearth of anything it is the human resource.

To be able to be productive and highly competitive society like America this human resource is of paramount significance. It is only the more gifted and talented members of the society who succeed in comparison with the masses. Since the natural resources and other human endeavor have created endless opportunities in various spheres, these call for talented and hard working people from all over the world. If America is successful today it is because of the joint efforts of these millions of talented immigrants from all over the world. In essence if people have certain innate abilities that needs a field for fruition, America is the land of such opportunities. America is not the land of people who are afraid of hard work. People who are endowed with superior talents, people who are not used to status quo, people who are rebellious or adventurous, America invites them to its shores, America want brave, intelligent and hard working people. Such people will not only succeed for themselves but also they bring great succees to the American society at large. That is why America wants you, if you fulfil these basic criteria.

Why Some Indians Do Not Succeed In America

Basically if a person is not hard working, he will have difficulty in adjusting in American society. One's work habit has to be such that he or she can take care of one's personal needs on a routine basis efficiently. Because there is no possibility of having servants to help you in the chores. One has to cut short the frills of comfort in life and try to be more efficient. Indians by nature, particularly the middle class and upper class families have learned to be over dependent on people like servants and assistants who are cheaply available. This, one does not have in America. So new immigrants have to unlearn some Indian habits like expecting others to help you and learn new Americanized habits to try to do everything by yourself as far as possible. You will be surprised how quickly you can learn to help yourself in most of these areas of daily activity. You can learn how to cook, how to clean the dishes, how to keep the beds and your room clean and you can learn typing, computer operation and even more sophisticated machine operations. You should learn how to drive a car immediately if you are not already a driver in India. Most Indian students do not have experienced of physical work such as working in the fields, repairing cars or any machinery or taking care of animals and cleaning and feeding them. Many of these qualifications and experiences will be called upon while starting a life in America and you should be prepared to do these things and enjoy them. If you do not succeed in these physical activities life in America will be difficult or more expensive. Most young Indians will pick up these work habits and ancillary familiarity with the machinery as time goes on. But you should have an open mind to happily learn these steps of Americanization. America is a vast country with great opportunities outdoors. It is a great pleasure for particularly Indians to enjoy these immense outdoor facilities which are clean, safe and healthy. The public Administration spends billions of dollars to maintain the quality of these outdoor facilities and it should be a great welcome opportunity for Indians to enjoy them. Sometimes one is reminded unhappily to see immigrant Indian families and children cooped up in apartments or small homes in cramped big cities without ever venturing to enjoy the outdoors in America. When they say America is beautiful, they refer to the natural beauty of American outdoors which is really wonderful. A period of stay for one or two years in America should give the opportunity to open one's eyes to these beautiful features of American life which can be enjoyed if one is active, healthy, out-going and open-minded. If one is not able to participate and enjoy these features of American life, to say the least his enjoyment remains very limited. Their baptism to American life has not taken place. They remain disgruntled and dissatisfied and critical of everything American, most of the time making their lives and the lives of their immediate near and dear ones miserable. Such people develop a kind of psychosis when they criticise everything American. They criticize the weather and climate and the snow and rains. They criticize the heavy traffic of cars and trucks. They criticize the heavy traffic of trains and aeroplanes. They criticize the thousands of acres of green forests of the national park saying how useful these trees could have been in India as fire wood. They criticize the sky scrappers of New York city or Chicago or any major metropolitan city of America. They criticize the under ground trains of New York city that transports millions of people, on a daily basis. They would criticize when they hear about the underground tunnels that bring the drinking water from the up state reservoirs to the city of New York for local consumption. They would find all kinds of rationale to argue against the American Society and its activity. These are the people who are totally antithetical to understanding and appreciation of the American Society and its efforts. They would find any reason to criticize anything American as if they have been given an assignment to write about all the bad things of the American society. Usually such people have an inner reason to be critical like this. That is the projection of frustration in their own lives. Such people may develop a pessimistic attitude towards life. They may have some chronic health problems in themselves or the family. They may have history of continuous failures small and big in life. They may have been subjected to discrimination in the society. They have developed a frustration psychology which makes them apathetic and unsympathetic to the whole world. Such people are incompatible to American life style. They would be frustrated throughout their lives wherever they are. They would frustrate the lives of others around them. These are extremes of examples of incompatible persons coming to America. But majority of people visiting America for short periods suffer from a psychology of "Mine is better". These people would change their basic understanding and appreciation, to a positive level atter continuous exposure for longer periods. The best method of Americanizing Indian minds is the education in the college campus for a few years. If the person is older it takes longer for him to change his basic philosophy of life.

Problems Faced By Indians When They Settle In America

Language

It appears that American Society presents different situations for the immigrant Indians. First is the problem of language. Indians though educated in colleges in English have problem in American spoken English. Most Indians do not admit it. Because they have been speaking and using this language for many years without being questioned. Their accents and pronuciation of various words are different and can be totally misunderstood by Americans. Some Indians speak English very fast and thus can not be understood. Some Indians speak English haltingly but with different accents with the same effect of not being understood. If the persons are young enough and make a conscious effort to remedy their delivery of language, they can succeed without much problem. Some have to take remedial courses in English, particularly spoken English.

Most Indians educated in colleges are somewhat self conscious of their ability and competence in English language. If they become a little considerate to the American audience and take some remedial classes they can solve this problem. Language usually is not a problem for most Indians. But the above deficiencies are real in many instances and if the Indian students make conscious efforts to improve their own performance the rewards can be tremendous in their classroom performance.

Colour

Most Indians represent various shades of colour of their skin. They range from black to almost white depending on the region to which they belong. Since majority of Americans are white, people of light skin such as people from Kashmir, Punjab and nearby areas and the hills pass easily in the American society without being discriminated. Other Indians would be subject to some degree of discrimination, particularly in the southern states. The entire concept of discrimination on the basis of colour has been made illegal by the Supreme Court and is fading very fast. With regard to this aspect of discrimination based on colour, the Indians also have to develop some attitude of accommodation. Although, it is illegal to discriminate these long standing traditions and conditions in mind can not be expected to be removed overnight by legislation. Indians of all the nations of the world have to be more understanding because of their own experiences back home.

VISA

Continuing in a legal status in America is of paramount importance for a foreigner. Therefore the Indian visitors, exchange visitors, student VISA holders and all other holders of non-permanent VISA should be careful that they do not exceed the time limits of their stay in America specified in their VISA authorization. If by accident they have exceeded the time limits they should immediately visit or correspond with the immigration office for continuing their VISA on a legal status. If you voluntarily contact the immigration office admitting that this was an oversight, but not intentional, then the penalty usually is waived. It is, therefore, advised that as soon as one detects expiry date of the VISA either expired or nearing expiry one should contact the immigration office. Then most of the cases where the stay has been exceeded unintentionally usually it is condoned. If the stay has expired for a long time it is highly desirable that you file your application for extension of the VISA through a lawyer. You must make sure that the reason for this oversight was genuine. If you have long term interests in VISA like possibility for applying for a permanent VISA, this becomes a stronger reason to remain within the legal limits of the United States. There are several publications which publishes the immigration laws and can be consulted in the local library for any guidance. For serious immigration matters enquiries over the telephone can be made to the immigration office for clarification. Usually the clerks at these information counters provide brief answers to these situations. For any other cases one can consult an immigration lawyer over the telephone. Very often many of the offices of the lawyers and their agents will answer your questions. If the matter needs to be further analysed the lawyer might recommend you for an appointment with him, which may involve paying his fees.

Problems Faced By Women And The Family

The women from India when they visit America for short or long periods have some special problems. Many of therri may have language deficiency. They may not have been educated in schools. It is highly desirable that these women who intend to stay in America for long periods should make planned efforts for improving their knowledge and ability in spoken and written English. There are several Institutions which offer short courses for this problem including some local high schools. It is common for Indians in big cities to form small groups or associations based on languages. This custom is very useful to provide a reassuring situation for these linguistic groups. But because they speak in their own language, people who are not trained in English do not benefit in that area. It is recommended that either individuals or these groups should make efforts to educate the women who are not educated in English. They can conduct themselves programmes for such women or arrange such programmes for them in local institutions. If efforts are not made in early days in America to learn English, the individual is going to suffer its effects throughout her life. One of the major factors of my decision to retire to India was because of my wife was not educated in English and I could not take the appropriate remedial action in time.

In India women most of the time are contented with the life as a housewife Cooking, cleaning taking care of children, entertaining guests etc. In America this life limited to domestic chores is less satisfying and less fulfilling to the lady of the house. This is primarily because she leads a moderately lonely life at home without any relatives when the husband and children have gone to work or school. Even if she is lucky enough to have some part time worker help her doing the cleaning etc., she still feels left alone. Therefore it is advisable that Indian women should have enough education followed by local American preparation for any kind of career jobs in the American society, where she can remain productive and busy. just like the Indian male getting satisfaction from his job in America. She must also join the American mainstream in adding to her life's enjoyment. Such a satisfied mother at home will fit the American life style more adequately. Luckily for Indian women many of them are well educated in sciences and medicine and productively join the American society with immense contributions. However, there appears to be still large number of them being held back from joining the mainstream of America, because they are satisfied with leading a life they left in India. However, when they wake up later in life that they have been left alone, it is already too late. In summary I feel that it is the Indian women in America who need to catch up more with the pace of American society than the men.

The women particularly have the responsibility of bringing up and guiding the children in their formative years. The husband should also make joint efforts with the lady of the house to guide the children. If these joint efforts are well directed the children benefit immensely. But if the parents have different opinions children become confused and ultimately suffer in their performance. There are many family problems which could be resolved in Indian circumstances that lead to serious situations in America ending in break down of the entire household. Unfortunately the rate of divorce in Indian families is high. The reasons may be incompatibilities which were considered minor in India and tolerated become major factors in equally vocal spouses who have no elders to guide properly. America guarantees equal rights to every one.

OTHER PROBLEMS: Dating

In general majority of the problems faced by Indians are similar to other minority ethnic groups, who arrive in America from all over the world. These Indians should not expect to see this new land as expansion of their own old country but should approach it with enthusiasm and inquisitiveness to participate in the American mainstream. They should make honest efforts to conform to the expectation of the society and not confront its population and its traditions. Only after few years of experience one can hope to decide for oneself how much of the new experience can be assimilated or rejected by him. In my experience of about forty years in America I have found my experiences in India and America were complementary for most part, if one approaches the situation with open mind. The older Indians have more problems in adjusting to the American society than the young and adolescent ones. This adjustment involves acceptance of new ideas and customs from America by these newcomers. This can bring in problems in the family because the parents and guardians who are usually older are deeply ingrained in Indian traditions and customs and do not easily accept the American situation. They want to take advantage of the American system economically, expect their children to do extremely well in their classroom and other spheres of activity but do not want the children to be Americanized in certain other areas. That affects their daily lives. Adolescents and young people of college going age have the same basic urge of mixing with their counterparts of the other sex. The youths mix openly and freely in the schools and colleges and other work environments, but are expected by their parents to restrain themselves and remain totally Indian in their social expression and sexual behaviour. This is an impossible situation for parents to expect of their growing children in America. This involves the concept of "dating". "Dating" involves meeting of young people with their counterparts which is considered open and honorable in the American system as premarital selection process. They make lot of telephone calls to each other, they meet individually frequently at work or after work and they go out on weekends and evenings on exploratory sexual relationships. Many couples engage in sexual acts usually with contraceptives. This custom of premarital dating and related behaviour have become very liberal within the recent decades. Very often this results in having unwed mothers and fathers. Some fathers accept responsibility openly, others do not and leave the entire responsibility to the girls. Many girls go through abortions and face other complications. Such young people involved in underage parenthood do not make success of their innate abilities. They become "stunted" in their growth socio-economically. This situation is very real in American society in general. But less so among the Indian youths. But this is not uncommon. So the parents and guardians have a right to be careful but they can not succeed hundred percent in restraining the growth of their children in the American way. It is a very difficult situation for one to live inside the waters but not getting wet.

Health Problems

One common health problem Indians would face in America is rheumatism. Rheumatism expresses itself in many forms, one common form being Rheumatic Athritis. This is faced by Indians in the colder climate of the north of U.SA. Some other common problems are respiratory problems such as Asthma. This condition is caused by exposure of Indians to variety of pollutants in the Air in closed environments. Heart disease and blood pressure are common ailments confronted by Indians in America. By and large high pressure of the American work environment and rich American diets could be complementary to cause these diseases among the Indian population. Fever of unknown causes that are very common in India are less common in America, so also gastro-intestinal disorder among the children. Mental problems amongst the adults are not uncommon, particularly in women of Indian origin. An extensive study undertaken in England has indicated increase in incidence of variety of mental problems in the women of minority groups, possibly the same holds good in American situation. Indian women of adult age, when they immigrate to America are more susceptible to this condition. Suicides among adolescents and adults have been noted in the Indians. Accidents ending in deaths are common amongst the drivers. Alcoholism the Indian population is not uncommon amongst the adult males. Special rates of incidence of cancer in the Indian immigrants has not been established.

Bribery, Crime and Punishment in America

Bribery in America is almost non existent for the common man. One should not attempt to pay a tip to people who are working in the offices and doing their jobs. Paying gratuity to a government employee is a bribe and illegal. You can pay a tip to somebody on the staff of a hotel or restaurant, to a taxi driver or even fo a person who calls for you a taxi. That is legal. Paying a gratuity to a government servant is highly illegal. One should be very careful of offering anything of value to such an officer, while one has some official dealings with him or her. If you develop personal friendship with such a person and have social visits or dealings outside the office, it is O.K., but there are certain officers and offices who are specially prohibited from public bribery situations, one should be careful of.

Such a prohibited person offering to meet you outside his ofice for lunch or dinner, where bribery situations are proposed can lead to very serious offences and can land the proposing party in jeopardy. Such a person can be arrested and tried for bribery of a public official. A public official is one who either works for federal, state or local governments. Therefore, Indians are warned seriously not to repeat in America their natural instincts of winning over officials through bribery. There was an instance of a highly respected judge committing suicide in one such instance in Long Island, New York. He was stopped by a police for speeding, when he offered twenty Dollars to the policeman, but the policeman arrested him for bribery. The judge committed suicide next day. There are organized groups of people called Mafia originating from the Italian word which means "the family". These people have dedicated their lives and the lives of their recruits to carriers of crime. For these people no crime is too big. Their objective is to achieve their goals by hook or by crook. They themselves are not afraid to go to jail or lose their lives. They also baptize their underlings in the same philosophy of "Do or Die". They have rankings amongst themselves. The chief of the operation is the "Boss", who has captains under him called (Capos). The Capos have soldiers under his command. There may be other sub-Bosses in between. All these people are called members of the family that is the "Mafia". They take oaths of allegiance by spilling blood of their own and swearing by it. The "Mafia Boss" has a bigger advisor called "Counsellor". He is usually a clean man is call open to give legal protection to the Mafia gangs whenever the law enforcement department confronts them. He is a highly respectable man in his profession and in his society. The "Mafia Boss" is usually most respectable person in his neighborhood. He is very charitable to many public causes. He supports the charities with local Churches, childrens functions and activities, societies of old women and other charitable functions. He is usually a highly distinguished looking old man beyond any doubts or suspicion of his under world activities. He only passes the final orders. When he needs legal protection he has a very clean and respectable lawyer, that is his counselor to advise him how to get out of the messby paying least amount of penalty. The amount of penalty he will agree to pay depends on the crime involved. This penalty may range from sacrificing one or more members of the Mafia to go to jail or be killed if that would end the story. Whenever the Mafia boss fails in handling the situation with the law enforcement people, he would also go to jail and be able to control his empire and activities from inside the prison. This he does by brroing every concerned officer in the penal system. Jimmy Hoffa was one such Mafia Boss who is supposed to have been behind the murder of President John. F. Kennedy. To camouflage the issue and confuse the whole world he himself was killed and supposed to be buried somewhere in the grounds of the meadow lands sports complex in New Jersey near the harbour. This sports complex which is situated on a hundreds of acres of land which were covered with fresh land fill before the construction of the stadium and other buildings. It is supposed to be the grave yard of Jimmy Hoffa. There seems to be no end to the operation of these Mafia King pins in most parts of America. In most big cities there seems to be one or more gangs. The Bosses supposedly meet occasionally about once a year to face each other with strengths and accept each others territories and rule. They were more powerful in the olden days when the law enforcement departments of the federal government were less extensive. After John. F. Kennedy these Mafia groups have been less powerful and less interfering with the Government and the public. But they do exist. Their trades are extortion, bribery, crime and murder for money. They do not care if they lose their lives in the process. Their methods to intimidate a person by any action which would convince him that they mean business. This may involve approval of contract for construction by a powerful business executive. Admission of a client's child to a prestigious school or agreeing to a settlement of legal claims to any vast property of land or buildings. They achieve this by "making him an offer which he can not refuse". For instance if the business executive has a son going to a public school, he is kidnapped till the child's father agrees to the deal etc. So their motto is "to make him an offer which he cannot refuse".

Other than above, America seems to be a society in full control of itself. There is usually adequate number of police in every geographic entity, village, towns, cities and the state and federal system. The policemen and women are paid respectable salaries and other benefits not to stoop to misuse of their office for bribery. All the policemen have guns at their disposal, they also have motor vehicles at their command. They patrol most areas in groups of two in a car. Long roads and the big highways are patrolled by single policemen in the cars. These cars are specially manufactured by the car companies and equipped with special devices of protection for the riders against crime by criminals picked up. They are also equipped with two way radio and computer system which can check the numbers of the suspected cars. They have also access to codes and phone numbers of the nearest federal police system, which can be called at a short notice to give adequate help to this police officer at the time of need. These police officers have the power to shoot at any person or car if he suspects the party of committing crime or not obeying police order. In contrast to the Indian police the entire police system in America is allowed to carry arms and authorized to shoot if necessary by circumstances. Not to kill but to stop a crime. But many are killed in the process. In many big cities like Chicago, New York, Philadelphia, Los Angels, Houston and other big cities, there are lot of criminals who kill or get killed by somewhat indiscriminate use of the guns.

The judicial system that imposes penalty on the criminals is also extensive starting from the village to the towns, cities, the state and the federal government ending in the supreme court. The death penalty imposed by any court has to be ratified by an appellate higher court ultimately ending in the supreme court. The Supreme Court has nine justices, who were originally approved by the Senate, after being recommended by the President. They serve for life. They can only be penalised by a process called impeachment, if 2/3rds of the Senate membership approved. Impeachment of a Supreme Court Justice is like the impeachment of the President of United States. The idea of only nine justices controlling the function of the Supreme Court is a misnoner. There are extensive number of judges of approachingly similar powers in the federal court system. They are distributed throughout the United State under the name of federal district courts. Each court has multiple judges with jurisdiction over several states. Big states like New York and California have several district courts of federal judges. These federal district courts are extension arms of the Supreme Court. These Federeal Court judgements are rulings that guide all other courts, unless they appeal to the Supreme Court.

The State Court systems in America have final jurisdiction on laws which do not conflict with the provisions of the Constitution of the United States. In such cases the appeals can be lodged in the federal court system. In a final analysis the Constitution of United States which gives origin to all the laws gives final authority to the states in matters that do not infringe on the rights and privileges of people of other states. It also guarantees human rights all over the United States. Its recent judgements have avowed to uphold the human rights of even non-US citizens on the US soil. Recent decisions by the Supreme Court has legalized capital punishment in appropriate cases.

Income Support Programmes In America

Social Security. Welfare System And Unemployment Insurance:

The huge Social Security system pays regular amounts every month to needy and retired citizens of America. This system provides a basic pension like amount for the sustenance of the individual and his or her dependents. These amounts are usually enough although tight to meet the expenses of these individuals and their families. But this system provides a significant safety net for economic security of every qualified American. Such programmes are funded through several huge financial pools of money for payment to these needy people. The primary beneficiaries of this system are the retired employees of the US employers, either Govt. or non-Govt. Anybody who has a source of income in America is a qualified member of this system and his children below the age of 22 that are going to school or college. There are other categories of people who can also qualify under certain circumstances. The social security system also pays for the medical care (medicare) of the elderly and their dependents with special rules for funding. This medicare system amounts to 2 hundred to 3 hundred billion dollars a year. It is almost as big as the defence budget of the United States.

The Welfare System pays significant number of people in America who do not have regular sources of income for their maintenance. These are people who have no jobs at the present time, have large number of children their income can support or they have certain medical problem which unsettles their personal financial security etc. These people can quality for some basic payments from the Government to support themselves and their family. There is another programme called Unemployment Insurance System which provides for regular monthly payment to Americans who had jobs for at least six months and lost them and are waiting for new opportunity. Such people can qualify for a monthly payment upto seventy five per cent of their average income for one year or more depending on circumstances. The amounts of unemployment insurance varies from one region of America to the other depending on the economy of that region. If a person is discharged from a job he can qualify for unemployment insurance of seventy five per cent of his past income after a waiting period of two weeks. This insurance is provided out of a fund jointly contributed by the employer, the state govt. and Federeal Government and also by the employee when he was in service. These payments can continue for a year and sometimes longer under certification from the Federal Government depending on the nation's economy. These three programmes summarised above provide for the support of various categories of needy people in the society so that they do not become helpless individuals.

The percentage of these people in the American society under all these programmes would approach fifty per cent of the population of the United States. Therefore, these social support programmes are essential for any civilized society for maintaining a basic maintenance of its needy people. Before anything in the world. India must provide social support programmes for its needy citizens.

A Word About American Election System

In American election system is undertaken through out the country on one day every year. That is the second Tuesday of November of the year. This is a holiday throughout the country. Election is conducted for all kinds of elective offices which fall due at the time. Elections are held for positions of town supervisor, County (District) legislature. various offices in the State legislature, including that of the Governor and also for the Fedeeral Legislatures including the Congress and the Senate. This is also the date when President and Vice President of the United States are elected every four years. Compared to the noise, publicity and violence associated with any election campaign in India American election campaigns are very quiet and dignified where discussions and deliberations take place. Publicity in the radio and Televisions and various meetings and gatherings are conducted without disturbing the peaceful lives of the local people. Most of these meetings are held in closed doors with broadcasting of the programmes by the radio and TV. In America basically it is a two party system, the Democrats and the Republicans. Majority of the Democrats represent ordinary people while majority of the Republicans represent rich people. Like the electoral roles in india they have also lists of people who are eligible to vote in a particular geographic area. They have registers of electors for reference if needed. Most of these electors are reminded a few weeks ahead of time, date and place of election. Only one or two Government officers supervise the election. They are helped by local volunteers from both parties. They are usually representative of both parties as observers in the election centre. A few local policemen are employed to keep law and order. The election booths are open from about 7 O'clock, from morning till about 9 O'clock in the evening. No publicity campaign is allowed in the immediate vicinity of the election booths. Except in the big cities the number of people coming to vote are as sparse as 10 or 12 per hour. In big cities such numbers will be 10 times per hour. After you are verified as a bonafied elector you are allowed to go inside the election booth to choose anybody you like. This you do by pulling down the lever against the appropriate name. These levers give your vote to the candidate of your choice and is counted electronically. At the end of the day the total is known. In national elections the time zone differential, from the East Coast to the West Coast, of three hours is to be counted. That means the results of California will be available three hours later than the results of New York. By and large the results of all elections are known by the mid night on the election day.

Malpractices in election process were common in some parts of the country, particularly in the South during the days of segregation. Both things are matters of history. There are still cases of fraud and other malpractices in tight electoral races which end up in the Court of law. By and large the, election process in America is a very tame affair compared to some in India.

President J.F. Kennedy

Within recent memory of the American politics President Kennedy stands out as a great luminary in the western sky. Like many important public figures in the world President John. F. Kennedy was assassinated in Dallas, Texas, when he was visiting the city in a motor cade seated in an open car. President Kennedy was elected as President only about a year and half before he was gunned down. He had developed a blue print for a better world and had served a warning to the Communist Empire, Russia and China. He resolved that America would go to any extent in fighting the spread of communism in the world. He had also avowed his policy of helping the under privileged world particularly India to remove poverty and disparity amongst its people. He had also held out hopes to come to the rescue of the suffering human millions irrespective of national boundaries. He was a just, kindly, intelligent, magnanimous and humanitarian person and a born millionaire. He was a great patron of humanity. He was a personal friend of Pandit. Nehru. He was a friend and admirer of India. He stood by the side of Indians and sent a warning to China in 1962 Sino-Indian war. I saw him at very close range i.e., within fifteen feet when his motor cade passed by the Animal Medical Centre while visiting New York City and was convinced that he was very very handsome. No wonder American women loved him and elected him as President by tilting the votes in his favour. If there is a worthy American to represent his country in the world affairs, he was ahead of all of them. When America lost President Kennedy the world lost a great humanitarian and perhaps most important and loved US president of the 20th century. Despite Americas history of glory and overall prosperity, the gun culture that took away life of such a great human being stands incriminated in the world court of humanity and justice. He might have contributed to a better world if he had lived. Many Presidents and powerful people have ruled many countries of the world but nobody has made a mark on the human history and shown the role of "the shining city on the hill" in a more humane and positive manner as President J.F. Kennedy. In my estimation he was the man of the century in the world.

United States Of America, The Champion Of The Free World

This part of the earth when visited by foreigners appears every bit beautiful as is said in the anthem "America the beautiful". It seems given this country in its original wilderness when it was partly occupied by the American Indians was equally beautiful, in its natural settings of the wild, trees, hills, mountains, rivers peaks and volcanoes. Modern developments have added many comforts and amenities for the human inhabitants but whether it has improved its natural beauty is an open question. It is very difficult for a visitor to see and know America in its entirety in his whole life, even if some people would devote their whole lives to sight-seeing in America. They still may not finish it. The vastness of the country is staggering. Its main land would measure about three thousand miles east to west and two thousand miles north to south leaving about, 1/3rd of the land masses out side but are still part of America namely Alaska, Puerto Rico, Hawaiian Islands and many other small Islands in the Atlantic and Pacific. The coastline which is open throughout the year on both Atlantic and the Pacific is huge, about six thousand miles long. Politically America has fifty states One of the states that is Texas would perhaps come to the half size of the undivided Indian subcontinent. The longest river in the world spans America from north to south and is known as Missouri Mississippi river. One of the highest building in the world is Sears tower in Chicago. The longest suspension bridge in the world is the Verrazano bridge in New York. The longest underwater roadway is about nineteen miles long under the Atlantic Ocean at the mouth of Chesapic Bay connecting Maryland and Virginia states on the East Coast. The highest suspension bridge in the world is at San Fransisco, the Golden Gate Bridge. The deepest river in the world is Colorado river. Many more natural and manmade features distinguish America in its many varied locations, but the most important feature of America is the United States of America itself in its avowed philosophy of liberty of mankind on earth. It has used its gift of physical and manpower resources to stand by the suffering, humanity against the tyranny of the oppressors all over the world in many wars which it had fought, not only on American soil not because it was attacked by a foreign power, but to liberate mankind on a worldwide basis. This fact was no less emphasized in the second world war, when the world's most notorious tyrant Adolf Hitler declared a war against the world to subjugate it. War is always unpleasant and painful whenever and wherever it is fought. But war fought for this bigger cause for the liberty of mankind is more desirable than peace. This was not only proven by America in the second world war, but by its future leaders like J.F. Kennedy who avowed to stand tyrants anywhere in the world.

    The vastness of the land and its people and its resources when mobilized for such a worthy cause proved as a tide against which there is no defence. American philosophy and its leaders have proved time and again that it is ready physically, psychologically and with all the other anciliary powers it needs to fight any such aggressive behaviour by any nation or a human being on Earth. This was a note of warning given by President Kennedy to Kruschev or any similar tyrants in the world. This warning still stands. America is powerful enough to prove this and thank God it is so because of its high productivity and natural resources of America supplemented by man made capabilities in various fields. America has always remained ahead of the needs of a complicated world where rival interests of various nationalities are on a clash on a continuing basis. The world is a better place with an America as powerful and peace loving as it is now. Yet it is ready to confront any real enemy of the human society in time. This ability of America to be able to come to the rescue and protection of mankind is the greatest blessing on earth.

Basic Philosophy and Behaviour of Americans

Americans are very practical people. They like to do things themselves as opposed to theories and advice to others to do it. They would like to do a small thing with success than to attempt thousand things with no remarkable success, This habit they develop from the very early childhood. American children grow up more individually than in clusters. They are more deliberative in their work. With nobody around to disturb them the children and youth spend time experimenting with any kind of tools. These manual and physical work habits have possibly been inherited from their forefathers like the

Germans and other European artisans who would spend hours and hours polishing a metal object to perfection. Americans have learnt many trades from European artisans. They are highly individualistic. Each has a mind of his own. He does not get easily convinced of a fact. He believes in the concept of "Show me". He is very carefree, not overly careful of what others may think of him or his behaviour. He often speaks his mind. He is not very cautious to analyze how his statements are going to affect somebody. He usually does not hold any malice against anybody. Since he is not malicious, he also does not hold any grudge or hatred towards anybody. He can give a tolerant acceptance to anybody who speaks his mind. Although he may give very opposite view point in a topic. He is hard working and usually expect others to do the same. He believes in democratic principles, although he may not have learnt them by school. He is highly vocal and may appear non sparing while discussing other persons' view points. He believes in speaking the truth and simple truth. His statements and actions are not conspiratorial but upright. He can hurt a person without meaning to hurt. He is less diplomatic. He is straightforward and believes others to be so. He is usually not a penny-pincher. Usually he is not over sensitive or antisocial. He is highly respectful to others but does not make a big ceremony of showing that. He is very informal in expressing respect and admiration.

These human characteristics are predominant, but can vary from person to person. On a general analysis one would find Americans, by and large, are compatible people with other human types. They are very flexible when a highly placed person can come down in discussion with an ordinary person to his own level. He does not have the ego of his position. Like a President of a University talking to an ordinary student in his office. The president of united states usually discusses very important topics with his distinguished counterpart from abroad sitting on two side chairs near a fire place. This is the typical informality America presents. This lack of imposition of one's high and mighty position on the humble is noticiable. It is un-American to be pompus because most Americans start out with few guaranteed frills in life. This contrasts with various economic stratifications of people in Indian Society. The differences economic and social amongst the people of India is very remarkable in comparison to the people of America or Europe. There is a marked stratification of life of people in India which almost follows the caste boundaries. People belonging to one caste live in one part of the village separate from other castes. This practice has continued for centuries. The basic criteria dividing Indian society on caste lines have continued even till now in the Indian Society. This is the biggest scourge of modern India. This social malaise has been rationalized by various shrewd arguments in the Hindu Society. This is the principal cause of lack of unity in the Indian Society. It has kept the society divided for centuries. Recently even the govt. in its various well meaning programmes to help the under privileged groups, such as for scheduled castes and scheduled tribes and other programmes for protection of interests of the Other Backward Castes have provided respect and rationale for these divisive forces in the Indian society. In spite of great value of these reservation programmes for various under developed groups in the society, these features should not be accepted on a permanent basis or for a very long period. If such protections continued for long their effect will cause permanent divisions and sub divisions in the Hindu society and weaken it. Indian mind is very fertile. Possibly it will be able to find a solution to this problem of the under privileged without destroying the unity and philosophy of the masses of India. In these last days of twentieth century where discrimination is becoming extinct from all over the world. Indian society should not rationalise and perpetuate programmes to discriminate in the name of removal of discrimination.

Medical Internship and Residency

Opportunities for medical doctors in America to improve their earning skills along with improvement in their diagnostic and clinical expertise usually begin with training programmes for young doctors as interns for one or two years followed by residency programmes for three to five years in respective disciplines. The internships are usually rotating internships in three disciplines: Medicine, surgery and gynecology. Some hospitals have internship in one or the other disciplines. This job of intern is very hard, Because he is busy for most of the day and the night carrying out the orders of his superior doctors for diagnosis and care of the patients. Their duties usually are for sixteen hours a day allowing hardly any time for normal family life. They carry out their duties under the guidance of one resident and possibly one senior physician. The life and health of the patient is of paramount significance. Nobody is over concerned for the comforts or lack of time of this junior doctor or intern. Therefore, he is the busiest person in any clinical department taking care of patients. He gets the medical guidance from his seniors such as residents or attending physicians. He begins with a salary of around thirty to forty thousand dollars a year. This varies from locality to locality. He is the lowest paid doctor in the department. When he becomes a Resident, his salary goes up by about ten thousand dollars in each year of residency that is completed. After this residency there is a position of physician which is called a fellow. The interns, residents and fellows all have to be licensed in the state where they are located. For the foreign graduates like those from India this is the second examination they have to clear before they are appointed as intern or resident. The first examination for the foreign graduates is FMGEMS administered by an agency in America under authorisation from the American medical association. This is a basic examination to test foreign graduates with regard to their ability as a physician when compared to those graduates from America. This examination is not taken by those Indians who have got degrees from American medical colleges irrespective of their national status. They are exempted from this examination. However, all foreign graduates other than the citizens of America have to take the first qualifying examinations which is called FMGEMS. After they pass the examination of FMGEMS they are elligible to apply for state board license in the state in which they intend to practice or enter into internship or residency programme. me. Most institutes or hospitals do not insist on having the state board licence from these foreign graduates who have pased the FMGEMS. Such institutions may allow you to take the state board license after joining the programme. In the recent past there was not any essential requirements for a foreign graduate to have green card or immigrant status in the USA, before enrollment in the internship or residency programmes. Recently many medical institutions have tightened the entry requirements for foreign medical doctors. In spite of these tight requirements many institutions and hospitals allow these foreign medical graduates who have qualified in the FMGEMS examination to enter their internship and residency programmes. Such persons without immigrant VISA or green card may have other qualifying VISAs such as H- 1 or exchange visitor VISA. But this group is a minority. In summary, in order to be elligible for entry into the internship and residency programmes in American medical institutions, one must have a green card and satisfactory compleition of the FMGEMS examination. The state board examination can be taken later on. At this time Government of India has made further tightness in making entry of Indian doctors into American medical system very difficult. They not only lack the centres for examination for the PFMGEMS in India, nor they allow Indians openly availing of such opportunities in the nearby countries like Srilanka, Singapore or Pakistan, for a medical doctor to succeed in sitting for one of these examinations. These doctors somehow go out of the country where they can sit for this examination which must have been pre- arranged. There are still a few lucky Indians who qualify to get green cards or other VISAs to go to America where they can take these examinations. Basically the medical graduates of India have to complete the FMGEMS examinations and be holders of Permanent resident VISA or other qualifying VISA like H-1 or exchange visitor VISA. These medical doctors also should through their society urge the govt. of India to remove the restrictions on the medical graduates to explore such opportunities in America, particularly at a time when there is lack of employment opportunities in India.

Computer Science and Other Advanced Technologies

One of the important technologies the world has accepted in twentieth century is the application of computers in various fields of human endeavour. The concept of computers was developed in Europe but perfected in America. Although developed in the first half of twentieth century, this has been perfected in the second half. Basically it began with high speed calculation of mathematical problems which soon began to be applied to various scientific uses. Within recent years computers have been found very useful not only in sciences but also in day to day applications of many functions of business and Government. Everyday new avenues of application of computer is being developed. Things which would have taken hundreds of man hours for calculation can be achieved by computer in a matter of minutes. Things which were almost impossible to be calculated in the pre computer days are achieved at electronic speed. The ability of these high speed computation are being utilized in almost all areas of human endeavour with great success. Therefore, a society will remain uneducated and backward if they do not have facility in computer applications. Luckily India has made a mark in educating large number of its youth in computer science which has been facilitated by their English background. A large number of young Indians trained in computer science are able to travel abroad and get good incomes making careers in computers. The opportunities for better trained Indians in the country itself are increasing by leaps and bounds. The strong mathematical background of Indian educational system has adapted itself to the application of computer sciences. The world is still in the early days of mass scale computer application. They believe that India will contribute immensely in the advancement of application of computers in various fields in the coming decades. It needs a sympathetic and educated Government to encourage these activities. It appears from the process of the computer application in the world so far that this omnipotent human technology will probably reveal during the coming half century its unlimited potentials in the fields of mathemetics, engineering and other sciences which have so far been limited in their understanding and applications.

Cloning

There are many new methods and technologies being developed in the world among the computer applications. Many of these technologies have benefited from computer uses. Certain very advanced technologies have to be theoretically tested on computer models. Many individual biotechnology have their own method of development and application. One such technology which is called cloning, that gives rise to progeny which are identical to each other and their originators. Such a cloning procedure may make possible development of identical animals or plants to be produced in a mass scale. Such identical animals would be programmed genetically to have certain specific qualities and features or produce certain secretions, in milk or meat, drugs and hormones essential for treating many human and animal disease. Association with and education of young Indians in American University campuses engaged in these advanced technologies can be greatly rewarding for both the students and the Universities.

AIDS (Acquired Immune Deficiency Syndrome)

This is a worldwide disease which was discovered only very recently that is 1986. This disease is a chronic sexually transmitted disease caused by a few viruses and have no known cure yet. It is common in America, particularly in big cities. It affects mostly the homosexuals and their partners. Since there is no known cure, once a person is affected, his life is counted in months usually up to five to ten years. During this period the individual suffers a great deal from many complications with other disease conditions. Billions and billions of dollars are being spent now on research on AIDS and the drugs that could cure the condition. Some drugs are helpfal, but have not been proven as curative. Those which are helpful are highly expensive and hence almost beyond the reach of most people. It spreads by natural intercourse with prostitutes, who give it back to her new partners. Most common method of spread of this disease is through anal and oral sex common amongst homosexuals. There are many highly talented people of arts and letters and performing artists, who are homosexuals. Therefore, it has come to the limelight. The world is much safer today after the significance of AIDS has been known publicly and there are efforts from many Governments and private organisations to control the condition, although no final cure or preventive has been discovered yet. There is a likelihood of high incidence of AIDS among the population of prostitutes in India, particularly in big cities like Calcutta and Bombay. These have been projected to disseminate the disease to the normal population at high rate in the future. There are ample opportunities for research on clinical and curative aspects of the disease in

America with open opportunities for Indians who want to pursue such programmes. There is a large number of grants and funds from various foundations available for such purposes. These offers are for basically doctors, paramedics and biological scientists, and provide great opportunities for research on AIDS. However, one has to be warned that this virus is a communicable virus under restricted circumstances and one should be very careful while handling the cases and the viruses.

Soil Conservation Programme

In America agriculture is the backbone of the country. It provides almost fifty per cent of its foreign exchange earnings. Agriculture usually is a huge and mass enterprise. It involves individual farms which are thousands of acres or thousands of animal operations. Its production are huge which results in large annual surpluses in each agricultural produce. Since a few recent years the world has been able to produce enough food not to need huge inputs from American stocks, America has recently found that it is un-economic and wastage of national resources to over-produce various agricultural commodities on a national scale amounting to billions and billions of dollars as the price of these surplus produce. Although they have been always calculating on how much to produce on each agricultural item, recently a national stock taking has given rise to recommendations to methods of conservation rather than over production. The net effects of these new policies of the United States are not to unbalance the agricultural market in the world but to conserve its natural resources for future needs of the populations of the world. Research on agricultural sciences and technology conducted both at national, state and private levels continue to asses the values of various measures to conserve its natural resources and potentials in agriculture with provision for time to time assessment of the needs to adjust production of any one particular item. Many specialised programmes have been developed in America to conserve their natural resources for agriculture. There is a huge division for soil conservation programmes in the department of agriculture, whose daily activities are to monitor various regions of land against soil erosion. They give major emphasis to conservation measures to prevent soil erosion. This kind of erosion happens in many instances and due to variety of causes, primarily due to water and wind. It is surprising how the American agricultural scientists pool all their resources and scientific and practical knowledge to develop plans to prevent loss of soil due to water and wind erosion. Indian agricultural scientists can tremendously benefit from practical participation in some of the programmes of the soil conservation department of the US department of agriculture. Just like Indo-Gangetic plains were built by the silt brought in by the river Indus and Ganges. Similarly some rivers carry away millions and millions of tonnes of valuable soil from India to the seas while distributing a few tonnes free of charge to the millions of acres of land in their paths. The Bureau of Research at the National Level on Agriculture called ICAR have a great role in this regard to conserve the soil of India where rainfall is very heavy in some months of the year. Many impressive techniques of soil conservation measures adopted in United States on a national basis were depicted in a hand book of agriculture produced in 1987. Summarised, many of these beneficial measures can be applied to India on a nationwide basis. Before accepting these methods of conservation the ICAR scientists will have to reevaluate their applicability in Indian conditions. I was very impressed to observe a few of the examples of soil conservation measures and other agricultural methods which are being applied in the fields in the Eastern United States.

Preventing Loss In Storage of Agricultural Commodities

It is well known that in India a large percentage of the produce is wasted in the process of storage. Storage of rice, wheat, groundnuts, grams, mung and many other agricultural produce are adversely affected by inadequate and improper storage facilities. Indians should see and have practical experience of how various grains and agricultural produce which are produced in mass scale in America are stored without much appreciable loss. Further, there is a loss of produce in transportation due to defective containers and other damaging causes. Insects and pests cause tremendous loss to the agricutural communities on a national basis. Our agricultural scientists can immensely benefit from practical participation in large operations of grain producing companies in this regard. Regular use of pesticides and insecticides also help. One is impressed tremendously when one sees the harvesting of grains in a large farm. In such farms harvesting of wheat, rice or barley are conducted by huge combines that crop the cups of the plant into a crusher which removes the grain individually that is pumped by hydraulic measures into the silos directly. A silo with a diameter of about fifty feet can hold the harvest of about hundred acres of produce. The silos are pretreated with pesticides and protected against pests for long period storage.

There are many newer technologies which are modified from time to time that are beneficial to agriculture production. These are recommended from the national research centres to be adopted by the farmers. It is very impressive to observe the cooperation, acceptance and implementation of the farmers with the Central Government service departments. These recommendations are sent out by the central authorities as bulletins from time to time.

Oriya Families In America

It is very gratifying for Oriyas that there are a large number of Oriya families settled in America and Canada. They may number about a thousand plus. Majority of these people are the extended families of doctors, educationists and research workers. Most of them particularly nonmedical people have doctoral degrees in sciences and literature. A few lawyers are also there. Amongst the professionals there are a large number of engineers, veterinarians and MBAs. The children of this first generation Oriyas are also becoming well educated in medicine, sciences and other learned professions. Large number of them have succeeded in entering into medical profession. This is a compliment to the Oriya children because their success in getting admission to medical schools in America needs high scholastic achievement. Besides, medical education in America is expensive and only affluent Oriya families are able to support the expensive education of their children. By and large Oriyas in America are a progressive group and have made a mark in the educated society amongst the Indians.

I had the unique privilege of having a number of distinguished Oriyas living with my family for prolonged periods of time as paying guests. I was lucky to have the association with these highly distinguished individuals from Orissa because these long term associations were mutually beneficial also on a social basis. This programme might have helped some Oriyas to get a little bit of relief from their home sickness because of living in our home and speaking in Oriya. These individuals included Mr. and Mrs. Saradindu Mishra, Dr. N.C. Panda, Dr. J.B. Das (Ex- Directors of Health), Mr. Purna Chandra Mohapatra, Mr. Dillip Kr. Satpathy. I am happy and proud of my past and present association with these individuals and their families.

It is only a few individuals from among the Oriyas that I was able to help to settle down in America on permanent VISAs. I remember only two instances where I was directly instrumental in helping them to get the green card. These individuals had their unique qualifications to justify their immigration to America but they needed a sponsorship and offer of employment which I provided. One was Dr. Amiya Kr. Pattnaik, Veterinary Pathologist from Orissa whom I sponsored through the AMC. The second was Mr. P.C. Mohapatra whom I sponsored through the Yonkers Animal Hospital. These worthy individuals are well settled in America with their families. I am happy and proud to have been able to help these countrymen legally who established themselves in America with their extended families.

Indo-American Charity For Orissa Cyclone Relief:

I instituted this non-profit organisation to collect funds for use as a relief against the ravages of a severe Cyclone that affected almost the whole of coastal Orissa in 1971-72. This Organisation raised some money and the proceeds of this fund was channelised for relief measures through the Servants of India Society, then headed by Late Shyam Sundar Mishra. This was a token help for the cyclone damages, contributed more by the American public than by the NRI's.

Osany Scholarships

Three scholarship funds were established by OSANY during my tenure as president of OSANY through the efforts of Mr. Manoranjan Pattnaik, Mrs. Jayanti Mahapatra and others. An Annual Joint Convention of OSA and OSANY was conducted where the substantial surplus income was generated. It was later on decided to use this surplus create three permanent scholarship funds in Orissa to provide Annual Scholarships for the best graduates of the University. In consultation with the University administration of Utkal University, Berhampur University and Sambalpur University three fixed deposits were made at the State Bank of India for this purpose. Only the interest out of the deposits was to be granted as scholarship to the best graduate of the University every year. The programme is still continuing thanks to the Oriya Community in America.

Baisi Mouza College

I had an urge to do some patriotic work for my countrymen in Orissa, where I was born, brought up and educated. In one of the meetings of some enthusiastic young people from the locality of Baisi Mouza, an appeal was made to me to found a college in the area because of its isolated and neglected situation. This area referred to as Baisi Mouza is an Island region surrounded by two rivers,

Devi and Bilua khai. It has very precarious communication facilities with the outside world. After a little bit of initial reluctance of adding more unemployed youths in the job lines I convinced myself that education is like giving the blessing of eyesight to the blind and therefore decided to give whatever support I could to establish a college of higher education in Baisi Mouza. Initially I gave a challenge to the local enthusiasts amongst the youth that I would match any fund they raised by local donation. With this challenge accepted successfully by the local organizers I joined hands with them to start the foundation of Baisi Mouza College with initial one lakh of rupees pledged to the Government for initiating the Baisi Mouza College. I also offered some additional amounts for the local fund raising effort for establishment of the buildings and acquisition of land etc. I am very happy that our initial efforts of acquiring about five acres of land and erection of a few buildings on the newly acquired land convinced the district administration and local politicians to provide additional funds for buildings and equipment which are continuing. The present programme of the college which has been operational for about five years plus included only +2 Arts, but buildings and equipment etc. have been acquired for Science programme in +2 Science level. Our efforts have been endorsed by a joint visit to the college by Mr. Bhagabat Prasad Mohanty, Minister of Higher Education, Orissa, Mr. Ranjeeb Biswal, Member of Parliament and Mr. Laxman Mallick, Zilla Parishad Chairman, on 12th November, 1997. It is hoped that the Government authorities will continue their support to implement this programme in the college.

Americans are Very Charitable People

We need help all throughout our lives in every sphere of our activity. Every individual needs help from all kinds of people in his life time. This help can be small or big. But people depend on other people in this area of getting help. Some societies are more forthcoming in helping each other. Some are less. This special feature of helping each other is very important in progress and development of human society. In my days in America I was most impressed with the helpfulness of individual Americans even to strangers like us. If you need any help at all you have to do is ask anybody that passes your way. If you are asking for directions to a new place, you can be sure that the person will try his utmost to help you. If he is driving and you are walking he will give you a lift to take you part of the way in your direction. Others will give you verbal directions, some may draw you a map with the names of the streets and the number of the bus you have to take to reach that place. Very commonly if a pedestrian is asking for direction from a driver, he is sure to get a lift in the car upto the place of his visit. Sometimes these places may be out of the way for the drivers. But the underlying factors in the minds of the driver are to help the person to reach his goal. This kind of getting a lift to reach one's goal can be extended to all areas of human activity in the American Society, which is a very important consideration in the progress and achievements of the society at large. I have experienced these humanitarian thoughtful and kind gestures in my life, almost constantly in the American society. Almost not a day would pass without experiencing one such episode of humanitarian help from my neighbours, from my classmates, from my teachers, from my colleages, from my villagers or from even strangers whose names and whereabouts are not known to me. This kind of experience makes one very proud and grateful to belong to a society like America. I used to get almost daily rides in the cars when I was walking towards my class at Cornell campus. When somebody sees someone who could use some help like transportation in car in the imclement weather of snow and rains they do not hesitate to stop the car and ask the pedestrian for a ride. I was getting free rides from my college town residence to my class almost everyday. I was grateful to the individuals who gave me the rides, but I was also grateful to the society at large that created this environment: an environment of plenty, the environmental affluence, the environment of relaxed mood that provided moments of thought of kindness and compassion to fellow human beings and the environment of progress and getting ahead yet without trampling over the feet of others. I would travel in America more confidently even in the uncharted territories with more confidence and less fear than I would in the streets of Calcutta or Bombay. I have made trips across thousands of miles of America in the eastern half of the U.S.A. along with my family and children and often without spending money in room rents. I must have visited in this trip 15/20 towns where I was guest of Indian and mostly American families. All I had to do was call up one or two days ahead of time to ask my American friends if I can stop with them for a night with my children and family. Most of them were overjoyed to have us as their family guests. They made no big impression to receive or feed us but whatever they offered us was more than plenty of food and other amenities. In this trip we visited one of the old acquintances, Dr. William Bone DVM, at Lake land Florida who accommodated us in his newly constructed animal hospital which had yet not been completed. He only represents a typical American who is informal but out going in entertaining his acquaintances and friends. I had known Dr. Bone when he was intern at AMC for about a year. But that was enough of an acquintance one needs to call upon American as a friend in need. During a family trip we visited Dr. Charles Rickard Professor at Cornell University with my extended family including my daughter and her husband, my two sons and my wife. We visited him in his home in the late afternoon without having called before. Mrs. Rickard and Dr. Rickard who had a huge ranch house in Ithaca entertained us with an afternoon party of cakes and coffee etc. They were overjoyed to see my daughter and son-in-law visiting from India. Mrs. Rickard asked if I had made my reservation in a hotel and I said, 'no, not yet'. She volunteered to ask us if we would mind staying with them for the night. I agreed readily and we were treated as honoured guests for the whole night. They took us for a formal dinner to a famous lake house restaurant on the shores of the lake Cayuga, where they had their boat. Dr. Rickard and Mrs. Rickard were very gracious hosts. At the time we visited, his large brood of children were away. Next morning Mrs. Rickard would not let us move without having a big breakfast of ham, eggs with coffee and orange juice etc. She also made sure to give us a few apples and oranges for the trip on the road. Mrs. Rickard was a very loving lady and was very affectionate towards my children. When I visited Cornell during any of my trips when I was at the Animal Hospital or AMC or with the Federal Govt. I always enjoyed visiting the Rickards for a few minutes. Dr. Rickard retired from Cornell as Associate Dean of the Veterinary College and had been my guide for my Ph.D. Programme.

Such stories of acts of charity and humanitarian help by Americans are unending. They are specially situated and endowed by God with the means of being very kind and charitable to their fellow human beings. This possibly has to do with their position of comfort in life which enables them to these charitable actions. These charitable activities of individuals help the society in a broader scale to grow and prosper without being over jealous of each other with enough space for individual activity and enjoyment. This is better achieved in a society with low population and moderate degree of affluence. One can not expect poor and under privileged people who are struggling to manage their lives with very tight financial circumstances to be very charitable. Helpfulness to each other possibly is an inborn character, but definitely modified by practical circumstances of managing one's life's needs with the resources at his disposal. The samples of America and Americans I have seen made me a true believer in the American dedication and passion for helpfulness and compassion, not only to fellow Americans but also the human society at large. Irrespective of whatever may be the rationale one is impressed with the level of charitable and humanitarian activities in American society, Charity and help to fellow human beings are possibly modified adversely in Indian society because of the straitened circumstances of the people. Over population, lack of social economic protective measures, persisting caste divisions, inadequate health care, lack of financial security for weaker sections of the society at large, lack of opportunity for educated youth in large scale are some of the factors the Indian society suffers from. In this area of human activities these are necessary and highly desirable. If one has to pinpoint any one factor as the most important

I would think of population as No. 1 area of concern for the future.

Go West, Youngman!

I have absolutely no hesitation to recommend to any youth of India to make every effort possible to go West, particularly I mean to America. This is not a shallow recommendation. It applies to Indians of all ages and geographic areas. Those who are lucky may be able to avail of this invitation. Others need not frustrate their whole lives trying to go to America but if they can succeed in their efforts to visit America for a temporary period even then it will be an eye opener and great educational experience. America is a new experience for human beings. It can be called a paradise which you may have in the dreams to achieve but may not succeed. Even then the dreams can also be very pleasant and sublime. America offers everything a human being can aspsire for in life. If he is lucky he may achieve most of his desires, if he deserves. Only by running away from the miserable experience in a poor country, one does not succeed. The most important thing one must have is a strong determination to do hard work. That determination which is like a seed wanting to grow all it needs is a fertile field where it can grow. America provides that highly fertile field, for growth of any human talent. In other older societies human endeavours are undermined by acts of jealousy of others who have been frustrated by not achieving anything. In America such people are fewer because they are happily busy in their own life's progress and stories of success small or big. They have no time for being envious and jealous of the achievements of their neighbors. Since everybody is usually busy in doing his own work either in the home or in the yard he has hardly any time to indulge in these thoughts of jealousy. They are happy to see their neighbors also busy doing their own chores. America respects those who put their shoulders to the wheel than the big armchair advisors. Those Indians who are willing and eager to lead a practical life not a sedentary life style confined to the armchair will find America most inviting. If there was a course of training for Indian youths for short periods of stay in American homes like six months to a year, I would like to recommend that very much in mass scale. May be the permanent resident Indian community in America would sponsor such Indian youth exchange programme for mutual benefit. In spite of all the hurdles in the path of young Indians visiting America for short or long periods. I would still strongly recommend to all Indian youth to keep the ambition of visiting America in their lifetime, even if it is for a brief period. You may not stay in the heaven for long but you have visited it, you will feel.

Index

A

Adirondaks 122
Adolf Hitler 198
AIDS 88, 89, 101, 207, 208
Akhaya Kumar 14
Alabama 17, 63, 70, 71, 74
Alaska 197
Algon Quin National park 120
American Ambassador 151
American Indian 116, 123, 124
American Universities 26, 28, 158, 160, 163
American Veterinary Medical Association 95
Amiya Kr. Pattnaik 212
Amrit Kumar 15
Anasuya 15
Animal Medical Centre 6, 84, 85, 92, 94, 97, 196
Annada Kumar 14, 15
Argentina 138
Ashdell 33
A University for Black People 71
Australia 19, 34, 139, 168

B

Baisi Mouza College 7, 213, 214
Bamadev Das 13
Basanta Kumari 4, 14
B.C. Basu 25
Bhagabat Prasad Mohanty 214
Bible of America 88
Bihar 14, 17, 46, 48, 53, 99
Bihar Veterinary College 14, 17, 99
Bimal K. Mohanty 11
Blooming Burg Farm 6, 113
B.N. Rath 25
Bombay 20, 147, 207, 216
British Veterinary Journal 19

Bronx 87, 94, 128
Brooklyn 87, 90
Bruner 5, 22, 57, 58, 59

C

Cafeteria 65
Calcutta 14, 20, 147, 207, 216
California 163, 191, 195
Cambria Heights 105, 107
Canada 18, 19, 34, 112, 118, 119, 120, 121, 139, 147, 152, 168, 211
Catholic Church 162
Catholic University in New York 162
Cayuga 5, 50, 51, 217
Ceylonese 70
Chamelli Mohapatra 113
Chashikhand 13
Chesapic bay 132
Chicago 63, 174, 179, 191, 198
China 139, 165, 196
Civil Rights Movement 71, 78
Cloning 7, 206
Cole 33
Colorado 198
Columbia University 88, 113, 162
Community Colleges 163
Congress Working Committee 78
Connecticut 102, 109
Constitution 124, 192
Cornell 3, 5, 14, 17, 19, 20, 21, 22, 24, 25, 26, 29, 30, 33, 34, 35, 37, 38, 39, 40, 41, 42, 43, 44, 45, 48, 52, 53, 54, 55, 57, 59, 60, 61, 62, 63, 64, 84, 85, 93, 102, 162, 216, 217
Cuban Island 124

D

Dallas 126, 196
dating 185, 186
Disney World 124
district courts 191
Dr. A.G. Danks 63
Dr. Banshidhar Panda 113

Dr. Basudev Pattnaik 47
Dr. Carmichael 98
Dr. Charles G. Rickard 5, 11, 54
Dr. Combs 49
Dr. David Detweiler 93
Dr. D.L. Coffin 85
Dr. D.W. Baker 5, 56
Dr. D.W. Bruner 5, 57
Dr. G.B. Singh 25
Dr. George Poppensiek 85
Dr. Ghosh 48, 61
Dr. H.B.Mohanty 20
Dr. Herb Rosenough 11
Dr. J.B. Das 212
Dr. Jha 48
Dr. J.H. Whitlock 21
Dr. J. M. King 11
Dr. John Beck 85
Dr. John Perry Combs 49
Dr. Johnson 19
Dr. Lennart Krook 5, 59
Dr. Marshack 85
Dr. Nimai Ch. Panda 113
Dr. N.K. Pattanaik 15
Dr. Pathak 48
Dr. Peter Olafson 5, 26, 55
Dr. P.P. Jha 48
Dr. P.P. Levine 5, 58
Dr. Robert J. Tashjian 11, 93
Dr. S.B. Tripathy 47, 48
Dr. Sitakanta Mohapatra 113
Dr. Valentyne's 52
Dr. William Bone 216
Dukes 20, 22

E

EIA 101
England 18, 19, 34, 98, 100, 133, 152, 168, 187
Europe 143, 201, 205
Exchange Visitor VISA 172

F

Fincher 22
Florida 6, 84, 123, 124, 125, 216
FMGEMS 203, 204
Fordham University in New York 162
Frank Reeves 115
Friesian 143
Fulton 128

G

Gandhiji's Quit India Movement 13
Ganges 209
G.B. Singh 14, 25, 99
Germany 34, 55
Gillespie 22
Golden Gate 198
Gracie Mansion 86
Graduate Advisory Committee 26
Greece 35
Guru Kelu Ch. Mohapatra 113

H

H-1 VISA 167, 172
Hans Bethe 33
Harvard 163
Hawaiian Islands 197
H.D. Srivastava 25
Hindu Society 201
H.N. Ray 25
Hon'ble Rajendra Narayan Singh Deo 113
Hon'ble Satya Priya Mohanty 112
Hon'ble Surendra Nath Dwibedi 113
Houston 191
Howard 84
Huntsville 70

I

ICAR 209
Indian Consulates 6, 174

Indian embassy 174
Indian Parliament 113
Indian Veterinary Research Institute 25, 53, 57
Indus 209
International Airport 90
Iris Yashodhara 15
ISCON 111
Ithaca 20, 29, 30, 35, 37, 42, 46, 51, 217
Ithaca college 42

J

Jagatsinghpur 13
Japan 167
Jersey 102, 143, 163, 189
Jimmy Hoffa 189
John. M. 44
Journal 19, 58
July 4th 136

K

Karnataka 15
Kashmir 181
Khetra Mohan Das 13
Kirk 22
Krishna Kumar 15
Kristina Rupasri 15
Krook 5, 22, 59, 60

L

Lata Mishra 113
Laxman Mallick 214
Library of Congress 45
Los Angels 191

M

Madras 147
Mafia 188, 189, 190
Maine 6, 102, 131, 132
Manhasset 4, 15, 107, 108, 109
Manhattan 86, 87, 88, 89, 90, 98, 105, 108, 128, 129, 137

Manipal 15, 106
Mann 21, 43
Maryland 132, 198
Massachusetts 102, 163
Max Plank Institute 55
Mayor 86, 87
Medlars 45
Meharry 84
Mississippi 198
Missouri 198
M.K. Gandhi 77
Montreal 120
motels 66, 70, 71
Mr. Bibudha Nanda Mohanty 14
Mr. Dillip Kr. Satpathy 212
Mr. Madan Mohan Pattanaik 11
Mr. Manoranjan Pattnaik 213
Mr. Naba Kishore Mohanty 14
Mrs. Jayanti Mahapatra 213
Mrs. Manorama Mahapatra 113
Mrs. Rickard 217
Mrs. Sanjukta Panigrahi 113

N

Naba Kishore Mohanty 14
Nassau 107
National Animal Diesases Laboratory 85
National Institute of Health 93, 94
New Delhi 147
New York are Princeton 163
New York City 6, 20, 29, 84, 88, 90, 92, 97, 107, 111, 126, 128, 196
New York University 162
New Zealand 168
North Shore Animal League 6, 98, 99, 100, 101
North Shore University Hospital 108

O

Ontario 120, 121
Orissa Cyclone Relief 212
OSA 112, 113, 213

Osany Scholarships 7, 213
Oswego river 121

P

Padarabinda Mahapatra 113
Pakistan 170, 204
Pandit. Nehru 196
Patna University 13
Philadelphia 101, 191
P.M. Academy 13
Port Washington 98, 101, 109
Pradyumna 15
Prativa Kumari 14
President John. F. Kennedy 189, 196
President Johnson 146
President Kennedy to Kruschev 199
P.R.K. Iyer 25
Puerto Rico 197
Punjab 20, 181

Q

Queens 87, 105
Quit India Movement 13, 78

R

Rajiv Gandhi 77
Ranjeeb Biswal 214
Ranjit K. Mohanty 14
Ravi Ray 113
Reverend Martin Luther King 71
Rhode Island 102
R.K. Choudhury 15
Rocke-feller Institute 92
Rockefeller University 88
Russia 139, 196

S

Salmonella 108
San Francisco 174
Sanjukta 15, 113

Scandinavian 104
Senate 191, 194
Shyam Sundar Mishra 113, 213
Singapore 170, 204
Sino-Indian war 196
Sloan-Kettering Institute 88
Smelting on the Lake of Cayuga 50
Social Register 89
Social Security 192
Sri Akhaya Mohanty 113
Sri Gangadhar Pradhan 113
Srilanka 170, 204
Sri Raghunath Panigrahi 113
S. Solomon 13
Standford 163
Staten 87
Statler Hotel 37
Statue of Liberty 88
St. Lawrence River 118
Supreme Court 69, 74, 79, 181, 191, 192
Sweden 34, 59
Switzerland 34
Syracuse 101

T

Texas 126, 196, 198
Thanks Giving Day 6, 106, 133
The Animal Medical Centre 6, 85, 92
Thousand Island 6, 119, 121
Toronto 120
Tuskegee 17, 62, 63, 64, 70, 71, 72, 74, 78, 79, 82, 83, 84
Tuskegee Institute 17, 62, 64, 70, 71, 72, 78, 79, 82, 83

U

Unemployment 192, 193

V

Vaijanti 15
Valentyne 50, 52
Vermont 102

Verrazano 198
Vinod Kr. Bansal 20
Virginia 132, 198
VISA 101, 119, 141, 147, 148, 150, 151, 153, 154, 157, 167, 171, 172, 174, 181, 182, 204

W

Wall Street 88
Wapingers Falls 15
Wappinger 107
Washington 45, 92, 98, 101, 109, 174
Welfare System 192, 193
White House 134
Wild Airport 20, 90

Y

Yeshiva University 162
YMCA 85, 86
Yonkers Animal Hospital 6, 97, 98, 99, 212

Black Eagle Books

www.blackeaglebooks.org
info@blackeaglebooks.org

Black Eagle Books, an independent publisher, was founded as a nonprofit organization in April, 2019. It is our mission to connect and engage the Indian diaspora and the world at large with the best of works of world literature published on a collaborative platform, with special emphasis on foregrounding Contemporary Classics and New Writing.

www.ingramcontent.com/pod-product-compliance
Lightning Source LLC
Chambersburg PA
CBHW060559080526
44585CB00013B/623